778.53 G559m   FV
GLIMCHER
MOVIE MAKING
                              9.95

JUNIOR COLLEGE DISTRICT
of St. Louis - St. Louis County
LIBRARY
5801 Wilson Ave.
St. Louis, Missouri 63110

MOVIE MAKING

A Guide to Film Production

MOVIE MAKING:

A GUIDE TO FILM PRODUCTION

sumner glimcher/warren johnson

1975 / columbia university press / new york / london

First published by Pocket Books, a division of Simon &
Schuster, Inc. Washington Square Press edition published
January, 1975. Columbia University Press edition published
1975.

Library of Congress Cataloging in Publication Data

Glimcher, Sumner.
  Movie making.
  1. Moving-pictures—Production and direction.
I. Johnson, Warren E., joint author. II. Title.
PN1995.9.P7G45   778.5'3   74-34300
ISBN 0-231-03962-X

Printed in the United States of America

Sumner Glimcher is president of Mass Communications, Inc., a producer and distributor of films, filmstrips, and audiocassettes. As adjunct professor of film at Columbia University, and manager of Columbia's Center for Mass Communication for ten years, he was involved in teaching film production and in producing and directing documentary and educational films, many of which have won awards.

Warren Johnson received his MFA from Columbia University in 1968. Since that time, he has worked on a variety of documentary and educational films in this country and abroad. He has also produced a number of award-winning experimental films for independent 16mm distribution. In addition, Mr. Johnson has taught film production courses at Columbia University.

All photographs in this book, unless otherwise credited, are by the authors.

FOR JOAN AND BEBE

The authors wish to thank Margareta Akermark and Mary Corliss of The Museum of Modern Art, Leo Dratfield of Phoenix Films, Ann Schutzer of Contemporary Films/McGraw-Hill, and Norman Lombino of Janus Films for their assistance and cooperation in providing the feature film illustrations. Our thanks, too, to Camera Mart for providing some of the equipment photographs, and to Bernard Barton for the illustrations. We also thank Erik Barnouw and Harold Flender for permission to use excerpts from their scripts, and our friends who helped in many ways.

S. G. and W. J.

Contents

INTRODUCTION

So you want to make a movie! Congratulations. Filmmaking is one of the most exciting, challenging and fascinating hobbies or professions there are.

To be a filmmaker is to be a magician. You make images out of dreams and your images become so real that audiences laugh or cry, shudder, scream or sigh, as you decree.

The professional filmmaker is the luckiest of people. He or she is paid to do something tremendously enjoyable. He is always learning, frequently traveling, constantly challenged, often exhilarated, and often deeply satisfied.

He may at times be very frustrated. An enormous effort in planning and scheduling can occasionally be completely wasted because of human frailty, misunderstanding, or simply bad weather. The risk involved, however, makes it more exciting.

This book will simply explain the basic steps you need to know to begin making films. The more you learn, the more professional your completed film will be.

To begin a film, you make a plan—just as a dressmaker makes a pattern or a carpenter a blueprint. This would be in the form of a summary you would write, called a treatment, or an outline with sketches, called a storyboard. It is a good idea to write more elaborate material, such as a shooting script, especially if you want your film to have sound.

Before you begin the actual filming, you must learn the basic elements of photography so you can transfer your ideas into visual images. Your first films should be silent; then, if you are more ambitious, you can try a sound movie. You can make a sound track either when you shoot the film or afterwards, and put it on tape. This tape can later be transferred onto your film so that your print will have sound.

Will your work be in Super 8mm or 16mm? More and more schools today have Super 8mm equipment. Some may also have 16mm equipment, especially colleges, where film is now often taught as a major. Both systems are portable, simple to operate, and readily available at a time when film has become an increasingly important part of the school curriculum.

Today we no longer communicate only by reading and writing, but more and more turn to video tape and film to transmit our ideas. In years to come, learning the basics of making and viewing film will probably become part of a productive adult life.

This book contains examples of film writing taken from actual films. The illustrations will familiarize you with the basic tools and help you to begin to think visually.

Film is a marvelous combination of art and craft. As a craft, film is based on the use of certain tools. If you learn to use these tools, you can do just about anything you want technically. This book will explain the tools. The art is up to you.

1. BASIC PRINCIPLES OF MOTION PICTURE PHOTOGRAPHY

---

origins • persistence of vision • slow and fast motion • film gauge: 35, 16 and 8mm

origins

The entire art and industry of photography is based upon two discoveries. The first was explained by Leonardo da Vinci (1452-1519) when he described the "camera obscura" (*dark room* in Italian). Leonardo was first to show how a tiny hole drilled in the wall of a room would, on a sunny day, project an image, upside down, on the opposite wall. The lens on today's camera corresponds to Da Vinci's hole; the camera body, his room. Thus, the camera captures the image and the film preserves it.

The second discovery is a simple photochemical reaction: certain silver salts undergo a chemical change when exposed to light. Strips of various base materials (tin, glass, cellulose acetate) were used as carriers of these chemicals. With the discovery of these silver salts, it was possible to make a permanent record of any given pattern of light and dark.

As early as 1727, these light-sensitive chemicals, or emulsions (skins), were painted onto rigid carriers to record images. Celluloid, or more precisely, cellulose acetate, today's carrier, provides the flexibility required for both still and motion-picture film.

persistence of vision

A motion picture is a series of these captive images taken one after another in a continuous manner. Each image on a reel of film is called a frame. The images themselves are no different from still photographs, each recording a moment of action a fraction of a second after the one preceding it. That these still images appear as motion or real action when projected on a screen is due to a phenomenon known as "persistence of vision."

Persistence of vision simply means that the eye continues to see an image for a fraction of a second after the image has been removed. If a number of pictures are shown in rapid succession, with each picture changing slightly from the one preceding it, the eye will see the changes as continuous motion. You can experiment with this yourself by flipping through a series of cards between your fingers. Draw a stick figure on each card in the same place and vary it only slightly from card to card. You can make it grow bigger or wave an arm.

Thus, the principle of motion pictures is based upon taking many pictures each second on a moving piece of film, and then projecting these pictures back on a screen at the same rate of speed to give the illusion of real action.

The intermittent movement of the projector causes a new picture to fill the screen while the eye remembers the first. The flicker of the first silent movies was due to the fact that successive frames did not replace each other quickly enough. The eye became aware of the dark interval that occurs during the time the projector replaced one frame with the next. All this, it must be remembered, takes place in a fraction of a second. A rate of 24 frames per second (fps) is now standard for 16mm and 35mm projectors. An 8mm projector will project film at 18 frames per second. If the film is shot at a corresponding rate, the action on the screen will appear at normal speed.

slow and fast motion

Projectors are normally fixed at the rates noted above, and their speeds are not variable. Most cameras, however, can be operated at rates other than those fixed for projection. What happens when a scene is shot at 48 fps and projected at the normal rate of 24 fps? The action will take twice as long to occur on the screen as it did when it actually happened. This effect is called slow motion.

The most common use of slow motion is to give a graceful or dreamlike quality to a shot. For example, the scenes of the couple in *Elvira Madigan* running through a field in slow motion give a heightened sense of romance. Another use of slow motion is in shots taken from traveling vehicles. A panorama taken in slow motion from a moving car will even out the bumps and look smoother on the screen.

Slow motion can also be used to examine in detail action which takes place at too fast a pace for close observation. Examples of this use include the slow-motion replay of sporting events as well as the horrific detailing of violence in the opening and closing shoot-outs in *The Wild Bunch.*

The opposite effect of slow motion, speeding up the action on screen, is achieved by shooting at a slower rate than the projection standard. If you shoot an event at 12 fps and project it at the normal rate of 24 fps, the action on screen will take place twice as fast. People or traffic appear to move in frantic, jerky action, and the effect is comic. Shooting at a slow rate from a car can give the effect of tremendous speed. Shooting at half-speed will make a car going 50 mph look like it's going 100 mph!

In the early days of silent movies, cameras were hand-cranked, and their speeds varied anywhere from 12 to 20 fps. When D. W. Griffith's great silent epic *Intolerance* was shown on television, it was projected at the normal television rate of 24 fps; that is, at a faster rate than it should have been. It is a testament to the film's strength that it was not ruined by the comic effect given—unintentionally—to many of the scenes by speeded-up action.

A special case of the fast-motion effect is found in time-lapse photography. This technique is used in the scientific study of the growth of plants and organisms. If a single frame is taken each minute, then the 24-hour germination of a seed will take place in a film a minute long!

film gauge: 35, 16 and 8mm

The gauge, or measurement of motion-picture film is referred to by its width in millimeters (mm). The big three are 35, 16 and 8mm. Until fairly recently, all Hollywood and most other professional films were shot in 35mm; some travel and educational films in 16; and 8mm was strictly for amateurs. Although 35mm is still the theatrical standard, wider gauges (70mm, Super Panavision and Cinerama) and narrower (16mm) can be projected in many theaters. Certain spectaculars merit the use of these new wider gauges (*2001: A Space Odyssey, Grand Prix, The Sound of Music),* and occasionally a director makes use of these gauges as a matter of style (David Lean's *Lawrence of Arabia, Dr. Zhivago,* and *Ryan's Daughter*).

Wide-screen effects can also be achieved with the 35mm gauge, as with Cinemascope, where the image is squeezed through a special lens when shooting and expanded for the wide screen through a special projection lens. Feature films, television situation comedies and dramas, as well as commercials, are still shot in 35mm, though in recent years features (*Faces, Endless Summer, Woodstock*) have occasionally been shot in 16mm. When this is done, they must later be blown up to 35mm in order to be shown in the projectors in commercial theaters.

In the past few decades 16mm has become increasingly popular, and today almost all industrial, educational, news and television documentaries are shot in 16mm. Because lighter, more compact, equipment enables smaller crews to work more easily and cheaply, 16mm production is replacing

(*Photo* 1) Comparison of Super 8, 16 and 35mm motion-picture film to a 35mm slide

much 35mm production. There are three to five people on an average 16mm crew: a camera operator, a sound person, a writer/director, and possibly one or two assistants. If the budget is tight it may have as few as two people, but no matter how generous, the crew size rarely exceeds six or seven. In contrast, a 35mm crew is almost never less than twelve, averages twenty to forty, and frequently runs over fifty.

Sixteen-millimeter stock is also less expensive than 35mm to shoot, to process and to print. The burgeoning of 16mm filmmaking has inspired manufacturers to provide better and lighter gear. In turn, the availability of better equipment generates greater use of 16mm film. In addition, finer emulsions with less grain (see chapter 5) and better color encourage 16mm use.

There are three kinds of 8mm film: regular 8, single 8, and Super 8. Since almost all 8mm equipment now sold is Super 8, and because of the larger frame and better picture it produces, we shall refer only to Super 8.

Super 8 is much cheaper than 16mm, in terms of equipment, processing and film stock itself. Super 8 costs only a third or a quarter of what 16mm costs. It is also easier to shoot because Super 8 cameras are smaller, lighter, and equipped with automatic devices.

Super 8 has some disadvantages. The smaller the gauge of the film, the smaller and simpler the camera, and the more difficult it is to achieve the precision engineering standards needed for the best picture quality. Since Super 8 records the same image on roughly one-third the amount of film required for 16mm, the Super 8 frame must be magnified over three times in order to fill the same size screen as 16mm. This magnification results in an apparent graininess in the film emulsion. Thus, Super 8mm film cannot be blown up to 16mm size without substantial image deterioration. Also, Super 8mm film cannot be satisfactorily duplicated in its own size to provide professional mass distribution.

Because the grain inherent in the film emulsion will be magnified to such a great extent, this prevents good copies, or prints, of the film from being made. The smaller size and slower speed also limit the use of sound and make simple editing procedures more.difficult, as we will see later in the book. Films released as Super 8 cartridges, such as educational films, are made originally in 16mm, then reduced to Super 8.

It is widely assumed that Super 8 is now at the state where 16mm was a few decades ago. Continued improvements in stock and equipment will undoubtedly encourage professional acceptance of Super 8 in many areas in the future. Meanwhile, its use is now growing at the fantastic rate of almost 200% a year!

What this means is that, for now, you should use 16mm if you expect your film to receive wide distribution or professional use. For fun and economy, stick to Super 8. The general principles of filmmaking apply to both.

2. PLANNING THE FILM

---

organizing your thoughts • visualizing your ideas: the storyboard • proposals, treatments and scripts

organizing your thoughts

Film is expensive. Thorough planning is necessary in order to use efficiently the film you have. Once in a while, providing there is enough material, an editor can rescue a good film from unplanned footage, but the odds are against it.

How do you go about organizing your ideas for a film? There are some simple considerations which have to do with the nature of the medium. No matter how many or how few people eventually see your film, there will be an audience. When you sit them before a screen, you automatically set up expectations. When the lights go off and the film begins, they will be looking for your ideas, your intention. Always keep your audience in mind as you plan your film.

Each shot sets up expectations and each changes the meaning of those preceding it. It is through this selective perception that you will guide the audience to your idea.

As soon as an audience sees the first few shots, the viewers begin to make associations. It is your job, as filmmaker, to plan a series of shots that possess *continuity;* that is, a number of shots that have a relationship, each to the whole, that together provide a story.

In a film we see a shot of X walking. Next we see a shot of Y. The audience now assumes that X has some relationship to Y and in your next shots you must make clear what that relationship is. This is called *resolution.* Until you resolve the situation, the audience will make assumptions. Your challenge is to anticipate these expectations and control the resolution. How you balance conflict and resolution is at the heart of planning the film.

Film provides the opportunity to dramatically structure an experience. As an example, let's examine the story of an early silent film. An old man is watering his rosebushes with a garden hose. The morning is calm, the garden pleasant, and the old man seems to be peacefully enjoying himself. Next we see a boy peering at the old man from behind a hedge. He smiles mischievously. We watch as he creeps toward the garden hose. Having reached his destination without the old man's knowledge, he takes the hose in both his hands and doubles it over. The water stops and the old man looks with irritation at the nozzle. At this precise moment, the boy releases the hose and the old man is drenched with water. Not able to control himself, the boy bursts into laughter. Now he has been seen by the old man, who halfheartedly chases him from the garden. At the end of the film, the old man returns to his roses.

In this story we can find a good definition of

dramatic structure. The old man in his garden presents the thesis and immediately arouses our interest. Conflict comes with the mischievous boy. Tension mounts as we anticipate what he will do, and the climax comes when the old man gets drenched. Denouement properly follows with the halfhearted chase, and the old man's return to his garden concludes the film.

For filmmakers, the story presents a special way of looking at the world. First we look for what interests us. Once we have found our subject, we want to know more about the situation. What relates to the subject, what affects it and what are the problems? Where are the mischievous boys?.

Now we can outline the film, develop the situation, and show its outcome. A good film takes the essence of a situation and, with precise timing, presents it dramatically to the audience.

visualizing your ideas: the storyboard

If your project is a short film or exercise of a few minutes' length, the best way to begin is with a storyboard (see Fig. 1). A storyboard is a series of simple drawings, one for each shot, arranged in sequence to show the development of the film. These drawings are usually drawn within a rectangular frame representing the shape of a screen. Beneath each frame or drawing of the storyboard, the dialogue or narration is written. Narration is a descriptive reading over the picture, such as that given by a news or sportscaster, and is sometimes called a "voice over," or V.O. Dialogue is the actual words used by the performers, as in a feature film.

In addition, you can describe important sounds. For example, a telephone rings off camera. You may want to add a few words describing the action within a particular shot.

The drawings can be as simple as you like, using stick figures with circles for heads. Their main purpose is to make you think about and plan each shot. In feature films, where much of the shooting is routine, this technique may be used only to chart crucial action sequences. But the shorter the film, the greater the story burden each shot must carry. Every commercial you see on television has been planned to the last detail on a storyboard. The storyboard technique is especially important in planning animated films.

The above storyboard illustrates a short sequence of two people meeting on the street. This would be a traditional development of the sequence in terms of the balance of shots. Shot No. 1 is called an establishing shot or long shot (LS). It gives the audience a long perspective and allows an examination of the environment. X stands, briefcase in hand, on a corner waiting for the light to change. We can see the building behind him and know what kind of neighborhood he is in. In shot No. 2, a second figure, Y, approaches X. This is called a medium shot (MS) and fixes our interest on Y's approach to X. Shot No. 3 is a close-up (CU) of Y's face as he asks X for the time. Shot No. 4 is a close-up of X's face as he responds. In shot No. 5 we go back to the longer perspective of the medium shot as the light changes and they part.

By changing the perspective within a sequence, for example, from LS to MS and from MS to CU, the filmmaker can fix the audience's interest on the significant detail in the action. What do you want your audience to know and what do you want them to see? For example, in this sequence, the first close-up is of Y's face because he is the first to

(*Fig.* 1) A short sequence: two people meet on the street.

speak when he asks for the time, and we would normally want to see the face of the person who is speaking. But there is something else. We are interested in Y's intention in approaching X. Is he a friend or a stranger, and what does he want? By seeing his face closely, we can learn much.

If this were a different film in which secret documents in X's briefcase were to be stolen, we might want to keep Y's identity unknown and a close-up would be inappropriate. Shot No. 3 might then become the hand of the stranger wrenching away the briefcase, shot No. 4 is a CU of X's shock and shot No. 5 an LS of Y's escape into the crowd in the street. On the other hand, Y might be an old friend and before we see his face, we might want to see X's look of surprise. In this case, shot No. 3 would be a CU of X.

Reviewing a storyboard will tell you where you need perspective and where you need to emphasize detail. Once you know what needs to be established, you can be sure you won't miss it. If you are not certain where you want the emphasis, you may shoot it several ways and then make your choice in the cutting room.

Take a simple event, such as two people meeting, and use it as an exercise. Change the significance of the sequence by the detail you choose to reveal. Use a traditional sequence of shots as in the storyboard illustrated above, then shoot the same event another way. Do it all in one long shot or entirely in close-ups. See what you think of the results.

(*Photo* 2) **Example of a long shot**   D. W. Griffith's *Intolerance*, courtesy of the Museum of Modern Art/Film Stills Archive

proposals, treatments and scripts

The production of professional films—whether they be educational, documentary, industrial or for entertainment—is usually preceded by several stages of film writing. The first written document is called a proposal (see example on p. 23), which describes the concept of the film.

A proposal tells what the film is about in a paragraph or two. It is customarily used to show to a potential sponsor. If interest is shown, the next step would be to write a treatment (see p. 26).

Written in a narrative style, the treatment further describes the content of the film: a treatment may cover as much detail as you wish—it may vary in length from a page to six or eight pages. It will show how you intend to approach the subject and will outline the style of the finished film. It may specify that the film will be shot silently with narration added at a later stage, or that it will be shot with dialogue, either as a documentary or dramatic film. It may outline a specific kind of music, such as a fast, jazzy score, or that music be used only as it occurs on location. It may note a need for sweeping, reflective photography, or rapid cutting from shot to shot of contrasting material in the style of a montage. In other words, the treatment should not only give a feeling for the final film, but should clarify your own thoughts so that you can communicate with the producer or sponsor.

In order to write the treatment, particularly for a documentary, you may need to research the subject of the film. This may simply mean a trip to the library or interviewing people knowledgeable in the field. Do not overlook previous films on your sub-

Kurosawa's *Rashomon*, courtesy of Janus Films

(*Photo* 3) Example of a medium shot

ject. Unless your film is to be shot entirely in the studio, this initial investigation should be followed by a location survey. This will enable you to scout for the best places to shoot, as well as to interview people close to the scene for further information or as possible participants in the film. Then, by the time you bring a crew out to film on location, you will be familiar with the places and will not waste time preparing for shooting.

The third step is writing the script, which is generally required for films with dialogue. For some films without dialogue—mainly documentaries—an actual script is not necessary. A careful treatment written after a survey is all that is needed for shooting. The script-writing may consist only of adding specific lines of narration to the treatment.

In making documentaries, much of the action often involves real situations and cannot be preplanned except in broad outline. In this case, the job of organizing the material, which usually belongs to the writer, is put into the hands of the film editor.

The final narration is written after the film has been edited. This is the case with the documentary film *North from Mexico*. Excerpts from the treatment, the draft narration and the final narration are given at the end of this chapter (see p. 22) to show the evolution of the film.

On the other hand, a film with specific dialogue scenes requires a shooting script. An example is the film *The Wild Child* (see p. 28), In such a film, dialogue scenes must be carefully contrived and worked into the film as a whole. A feature, or full-length, film is usually considered a sequence of dialogue and action situations, and is almost always written into the form of a shooting script.

A treatment may leave much of the content described in general outline, whereas a script is specific. The single most important feature that

Truffaut's *Jules and Jim*, courtesy of Janus Films

(*Photo* 4) Example of a close-up

(*Photos* 5, 6, 7, 8) An example of a dramatic narrative sequence: (top left) a long shot establishes the location and performers; (bottom left) a close-up of a girl watch-ing; (top right) a close-up of a child jumping from the swing; (bottom right) reaction shot. The storyboard tech-nique makes the filmmaker think in terms of precise visual elements.

distinguishes it from a treatment is that it contains dialogue, dialogue that will be rehearsed by actors or a narrator and finally recorded:

JIM
I want to read you something I wrote.
JULES
Certainly.
JIM
Promise you won't laugh?
JULES
Not at all.

Besides dialogue, a final shooting script describes sets, stage business and camera directions in great detail. It is usually written in collaboration with the director. Unfortunately, when the scripts of important films, such as Bergman's collected screenplays, are published for general reading, they are usually not in the form of the shooting script, which would be wonderfully instructive; they read more like plays.

A Proposal

MEMENTO *

A Safety Education Film

Many safety education films of recent years have produced so much anxiety in trying to prevent anxiety that they have had little impact. The so-called positive approach is too often flabby and meaningless. We would like this film to have strong impact in the way that the *Reader's Digest* article of years ago—"And Sudden Death"—had strong impact. We feel this can be done without having the numbing effect that should be avoided.

The basic raw material of our film will be the wrecked car and the business that has grown up around its collection, disassembly, and deprocessing. This material is of course macabre and could be horrible if used in conjunction with shots of mangled bodies. But our first rule will be that we shall not show injured people. We shall not show an accident. Our purpose will be to make the audience imagine the accident.

As we see cars being hauled to the "boneyard," stacked neatly in huge piles at transportation depots, disassembled into vast collections of tires, hubcaps, and other parts, we shall occasionally hear voices. They will be voices of teen-agers. They will be heard in carefree dialogue that will suggest the high-spirited outing: joking, bantering, love-making. It is the kind of dialogue that might have taken place in the cars we are seeing, before there was any inkling

---

*Written by Erik Barnouw

of the moment of terror. We shall hear the talk that went on *before*, while seeing what came *after*. What happened in between will be left to the viewer to imagine. A jazz score will be used.

The film will, in construction, proceed in a somewhat familiar documentary manner. It will tell us that the handling of smashed cars has become big business. We shall follow its procedures, in the way that assembly lines have been followed in other films, except that we shall here be following disassembly.

The automobile boneyard has rapidly become a familiar sight all over the United States. Driving through even the most peaceful Vermont valley, one can suddenly come upon a sweeping vista of crumpled hulks. On the edges of various cities are transportation depots where such hulks are stacked twelve deep, waiting to be moved to disassembly points. The stripping and compression of these hulks, at special processing centers, is a sight that is especially chilling in that it involves property that symbolizes prestige and pleasure, especially among teen-agers.

We have seen no film that has made effective use of this dramatic material of our time. Perhaps producers have shied away from it because it is "strong medicine." We want to use it precisely for that reason. But it must be used with taste and imagination, to stir the imagination and not merely to horrify.

The documentary thread that runs though our film will perhaps yield a final curtain. We might make clear, at several points, that the handling of the wrecked car has become big enterprise. At the end we might repeat this, using words to this effect: "However, its sources of supply are uncertain. And that, of course, is up to you."

While the material we shall use in this film appears to fascinate young and old equally, we should keep in mind that our central target is the teen-ager. In the selection of visual detail, music, and dialogue, we should address ourselves to his interests, moods, values, language.

Target uses: theater, television, school, film society.

Excerpt from Detailed Treatment

NORTH FROM MEXICO*

The film will open with a montage of contemporary Chicanos in confrontation with the Establishment. The scenes SHOT LIVE include the march from the Mexican border to the State Capitol in Sacramento of the Chicano Moratorium Committee organized by Rosalio Munoz and the Brown Berets in El Paso, activists of the organizing committee of Caesar Chavez's Farm Workers Union. From STOCK FOOTAGE and STILLS we may select riot scenes between the Chicanos and the Los Angeles police, and scenes involving activities of Reies Tijerina. INTERCUT: posters of CHICANO POWER . . . LA RAZA . . . etc., on the walls of the MECHA office at the University of Texas in El Paso; covers of Chicano student magazines, such as *El Grito* and *Nosotros*: Anglo and Spanish-language newspaper headlines relating to present Chicano militancy.

Our Narrator will be a Chicano; the music will be Spanish. Over the above opening montage the Narrator informs us that for the Chicanos of today mañana is yesterday. We're in a hurry now, he tells us, and it's very late. Maybe too late.

---

*Written by Harold Flender

It is over the opening montage that the Narrator defines for us Chicanos as Mexican-Americans, pointing out that nobody knows for sure the origin of the word *Chicano*. The most likely theory is that it comes from the word *Mexicano*. From its pronunciation as *Mechicano*, comes *Chicano* (*k* sound) to Chicano (*ch* sound).

But, continues the Narrator, while we may not know for sure where the word Chicano comes from, we do know for sure where the people come from. They are descendants of the great Mayan and Aztec civilizations. They come now, as they have for four hundred years, North from Mexico.

Opening Titles

We see thousands of Mexicans pouring over the Pasa del Norte Bridge from Juarez into El Paso early in the morning. This will be shot with long lenses from the El Paso side of the bridge, and, in addition to ESTABLISHING and MEDIUM shots, we should get many CLOSE-UPS of faces.

Over landscapes of the Southwest the Narrator tells of the first Europeans to arrive in the New World: Columbus, Magellan, Balboa, Cortez, Coronado, De Soto. We learn how from their base in the Indies, the Spaniards had, by 1525, explored the entire shoreline from Cape Breton to Cape Horn, and how an ill-fated expedition to explore Florida in 1528 resulted in Cabeza de Vaca and Estavan, a black Moor slave, being shipwrecked on an island. . . .

Excerpt from First Draft of Script

NORTH FROM MEXICO

Narrator

Mexican-Americans. . . . They call themselves Chicanos. . . . A Spanish-language minority who for years would say of themselves: "We are the best-kept secret in America." But they are no longer a secret. Suddenly, the entire nation has discovered the second largest minority group in the United States . . . the Mexican-Americans . . . the Chicanos.

Nobody knows for sure the origin of the word Chicano. The most likely theory is that it comes from the Spanish for Mexican . . . Mechicano . . . Me*chicano* . . . Chicano.

While nobody knows for sure where the word Chicano comes from, we do know for sure where the people come from. They are the descendants of the great Spanish Conquistadores. They are the descendants of the magnificent Mayan and Aztec civilizations.

They come now, as they have for over four hundred years, North from Mexico. They were already very much a part of the landscape when the Anglo-Americans first came to the Southwest.

They have been treated by the Anglo-Americans very much like another group here before them—the American Indians. They have been treated as second-class citizens.

In the early 1950s, the Negro civil rights movement began to emerge. At the same time, a new political awareness and self-consciousness began to develop among the Chicanos. There was progress in many areas. At the University of Texas in El Paso, over half the students are Chicanos. The faculty, however, is still overwhelmingly Anglo-American.

The Chicanos of today want to be treated as first-class citizens, and they want that treatment *now*. For the Chicanos of Today, mañana is too late . . . mañana is yesterday!

Excerpt from Final Version of Script

NORTH FROM MEXICO

Chicano. Mejicano. Mexican-American.
By whatever name.
They have long been one of America's forgotten minorities.
Its second largest minority.

OPENING
MONTAGE

They are descendants of the ancient Mayan and Aztec civilizations. The offspring of Quetzalcoatl, Montezuma . . . children of the Plumed Serpent.

CHICANO
FACES

And they are descendants of the Spanish Conquistadores, the searchers for gold.

COWBOYS

Mejicano. Chicano. Mexican-American. Today they will no longer allow themselves to be forgotten.

FAMILY
PARADE

They come now . . . as they have for over four hundred years . . . North from Mexico.
They were already there when the Anglos first came to the Southwest.

BORDER
BRIDGE

The Anglos have treated them as they've treated another group that was also there, the American Indians.

GUNS IN WINDOWS

In the early 1950s, blacks began demanding more insistently rights long denied them—human rights. At the same time, Chicanos began speaking with a new political awareness and self-concern.

BROWN BERETS

The Chicanos of today want to be treated as first-class citizens, and they want that treatment *now*.

For the Chicanos of today, mañana is too late . . . mañana is yesterday!

Excerpt from a Shooting Script

THE WILD CHILD *

Setting the Scene

A forest in the district of Aveyron.
Exterior dawn.

Fade up showing a peasant woman squatting and gathering mushrooms at the foot of the trees in the forest. She puts the mushrooms into a wide, shallow basket that she is carrying on her arm. She is in her fifties. She is making her way toward us. Suddenly, against the gentle rustling and the continuous chirping around her, she hears a different sound, as of a cracking branch. She stops walking and, puzzled, turns around in the direction of the noise. She looks up.

Leaves are moving, although there is no wind; abstract shadows produced by the sun's rays suddenly seem to be stirring. The peasant woman listens, then resumes her work, gathering mushrooms and placing them carefully into her basket. She goes to another tree, bends down . . . and suddenly she hears a louder crack of a branch. She stands up again quickly, examining everything around her with a puzzled look on her face.

A few feet away from her she sees several branches near the ground which are moving, and some form

---

of creature—man or beast—becomes noticeable in the dappling sunlight. Under the branches, this "animal," with a strange panting, is scratching the earth and sending it flying into the air.

Although anxious, the woman is still staring at her unusual apparition. Through the flying leaves and dirt, she now perceives the black shape of a curious animal. Frightened, she drops her basket of mushrooms and runs off.

We *close up* to the object of her fright: It is a child, about twelve years old: The Wild Child. He is naked, with scars all over his body. His hair is black and very long, his face even blacker with filth than his body. His nostrils are quivering, and seem to enlarge as if he were scenting something. We follow him. In two or three swift leaps, he moves over to the spot where the basket of mushrooms is spilled on the ground.

The wild boy is now on all fours in front of the basket and the mushrooms, which he sniffs suspiciously. Then he stuffs a handful of them into his mouth, half crushing them against his face as he does so. As he eats, his eyes move constantly all around.

We *close up* slowly toward him as he goes on eating and smearing his face with mushrooms, still squatting. Now he runs down to the stream. There, flat on his belly on a rock, he stretches his face toward the clear running water and drinks as some animals do. After drinking, he strokes the surface of the water and resumes his running through the branches. Suddenly, he stops, rising to a nearly upright position; his muscles tense, like an animal on the alert. And ceaselessly his eyes shift from right to left and back again. In successive leaps, he reaches the foot of a tree and climbs it, as nimbly and quickly as a monkey. He digs his nails like claws into the bark to help himself up.

Dancing sunlight through the leaves and branches. View of the wild child among the foliage. He is watching, scratching his head and body. Leaning back against the trunk of the tree, he rocks himself forward and backward.

Zoom out very slowly, revealing the forest. *Iris out.*

Dialogue

Dr. Itard's office.
Interior day.

Itard is standing in front of his writing stand. He is writing with a quill pen. *Voice over* of the text he is writing.

COMMENTARY *(V. O.): All over Paris there is talk of nothing but the child captured in the forest, who has been nicknamed "The Wild Child of Aveyron." Public curiosity is at its height, and my learned colleagues Cuvier and Sicard have obtained authority from the Minister of the Interior, Champagny, to transfer him to Paris. The papers relate that after an attempted escape the young savage has been recaptured and is at present secured in the gendarmerie at Rodez.*

Police station at Rodez.
Interior day.

Near the door, there are two policemen posted. In a corner of the room, there is a caged cell. Behind the bars, we can see the wild child huddled up. He is wearing a ragged old frock. He is still as dirty as before and whimpering.

The Commissioner is sitting behind his desk facing us. He is talking to Old Rémy, whose back is toward us.

COMMISSIONER: The orders from Paris are explicit. We must leave this week. Here, come with me.

We follow the Commissioner up to the door of the caged cell, which he opens. The wild child is still squatting, huddled up. He is moaning weakly. The Commissioner enters, followed by Rémy.

COMMISSIONER: He can't go like that!

The Commissioner walks back and forth in the cell, looking at the child.

COMMISSIONER: He's filthy! He stinks!

Passing in front of Rémy, the Commissioner steps out to get a sponge from the shelf; then he comes back, grabs a jug of water, pours some on the sponge and goes toward the wild child, who springs up furiously and fights him off violently, striking the Commissioner.

COMMISSIONER (furious): Ouch! The dirty pig!

Rémy bounces toward the Commissioner, who has pushed himself away from the wild child, and takes the sponge.

RÉMY: Let me do it. He's calmer with me. He knows me.

Rémy's hand gently parts the child's hair, which

almost covers his face, and he slowly washes his cheeks, forehead, and mouth with the sponge. The child is now docile in front of the old gentle-eyed man.

Iris out.

summary

A well-made film is the product of much planning. Even a documentary which is not scripted is still the subject of much forethought. Robert Flaherty, the father of the documentary, spent years living in the Hudson Bay region studying Eskimo life before making *Nancok of the North.* The more easily and smoothly the film flows, the more planning went into it. Do as much work as you possibly can before you expose one foot of film.

3 THE MOTION PICTURE CAMERA

---

transport • threading • film capacity • shutter • single-framing • projector • viewfinder • lens mount • filter slot • camera noise • motors and power

The motion-picture camera is the basic tool for film. Although its cost may range from $50 (Super 8) to $50,000 (35 or 70mm), all movie cameras do essentially the same thing and in much the same way.

Imagine the camera as a box with two primary functions. The first is to capture an image and bring that image to a point of focus inside the camera. The second is to feed a long strip of film through a flat gate positioned just where the image brought inside is focused. This chapter will deal with the second function and the next chapter will take up the subject of lenses.

transport

The system that moves the film through the camera is called the film transport. It begins with a spindle upon which a spool of raw stock, or unexposed film, is placed. This is called the "feed spool." The transport system ends with a "take-up spool" upon which the exposed film is wound. In between is the gate where the film will be exposed.

In 16mm and larger gauges, the film is loaded by hand. The film is threaded through two or more sprocketed rollers and the gate.

In Super 8, threading is much simpler. Modern Super 8 cameras are equipped with cartridge loading so that to load, a cartridge is simply snapped into place. Feed, take-up and gate positioning are all accomplished automatically.

The whole secret of how motion-picture filming works lies in the two words, *intermittent motion.* This is the manner in which the strip of film moves through the gate. Instead of a steady, continuous flow of film, just as it comes off the feed spool, the film is stopped an instant before the shutter is opened. Then the shutter opens and one image is captured on a stationary frame. The shutter closes again long enough for the strip of film to be pulled down one frame—just enough to clear the length of film where the last image was exposed—and the next frame is brought into place. The shutter is opened again, and this process is repeated 24 times every second.

The film must pass through the gate with intermittent motion so that it will remain still each instant the shutter opens. Because of the difference in the smooth motion of the film at the feed

Photos courtesy of Camera Mart

(*Photos* 9, 10) Two Super 8 cameras: the Bolex and the Beaulieu and take-up reels compared with the jerky motion at the gate, two loops are formed in the film, one on either side of the gate. The sole purpose of these loops is to enable the film to flex sufficiently so that these two different motions (1. continuous; 2. intermittent) can flow, one into the other, without tearing or straining the film.

threading

The cameraman's first job is to load the camera. If you are working with Super 8, this means simply opening up the camera and inserting a cartridge. With 16mm cameras, the film must be threaded. To do this, consult the threading diagram for your particular camera.

Figure 2 shows a common transport and threading diagram. Coming off the feed spool, the first few feet of film are engaged in a sprocketed drive. Then the first loop is formed and the film is inserted in the camera gate (C). After the gate is closed, a second loop is formed and the film is engaged in a second sprocket drive. At this point, you should have at least a foot of film left so that the free end can be securely inserted and wound onto the take-up spool.

Remember when forming the loops that they should be large enough to permit the intermittent movement of the film in the area of the gate, but not so large that the film rubs against the inside of the camera housing.

After threading, with the camera still open, operate the camera motor momentarily by depressing the camera's turn-on switch. This will tell you whether you have threaded it correctly. Check to make sure the film is taut while winding around the

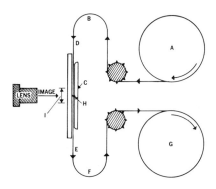

(*Fig. 2*) A typical threading diagram: A—feed spool; B—feed loop; C—gate and pressure plate; D to E—film plane; F—take-up loop; G—take-up spool; H—pull-down claw; I—aperture.

(*Photos* 11, 12, 13, 14) Four widely used 16mm cameras: (upper left) the Beaulieu 16, (lower left) the Eclair NPR, (upper right) The Eclair ACL, (lower right) the Arriflex S

take-up spool. Replace the camera cover and lock it shut. Make sure that it fits tightly so there will be no light leakage.

As the film passes through the gate (C), a small, pull-down claw (H) moves forward and engages one sprocket hole. The pull-down claw moves downward precisely one frame, pulling the film with it. It withdraws from the sprocket hole just as the shutter opens, and while this particular frame is being exposed, the pull-down claw moves up to engage the next sprocket hole. It does so just as the shutter closes again, and the cycle is repeated 24 times each second for 16mm or 35mm normal speed, and 18 times each second for Super 8mm normal speed.

In most 16mm cameras used professionally, and in all 35mm cameras, one or two registration pins move into the sprocket holes of the film during the time the shutter is open. The registration pin locks each frame into place after the pull-down claw has moved the film down. Immediately after the frame has been exposed, the registration pin withdraws so that the pull-down claw can bring the next frame into position. This insures rock-steady registration during the time the frame is exposed. In Super 8 and less expensive 16mm cameras, the film is held steady by friction. The pressure from a spring in the gate area is sufficient to hold the film steady while the claw is withdrawn.

The film running from D to E is held flat by the pressure of the gate (C). The area between D and E is called the film plane. In front of the gate (C) and in the area of the claw (H) is an opening in the camera housing the size of one frame (I), which admits the light from the lens onto the film emulsion. This is called the camera aperture. Before threading the film, make sure this area is free from dust or dirt. Dust can be blown free. If a deposit of tiny particles of film emulsion has built up in the

(*Photo* 15) Threading the Arri S. Film feeds off top spool, passes through sprocketed rollers to gate (shown open) and then passes through second set of sprocketed rollers to take-up spool (shown on table).

area of the gate, remove this with a cloth or a wooden pick. Never use anything sharp or metallic to clean inside the camera body.

film capacity

The standard Super 8 camera holds a 50-foot cartridge of film, which runs for $3^1/_3$ minutes. Sixteen-millimeter cameras not designed for shooting with sound take 100-foot daylight loading spools of film, which run for $2^3/_4$ minutes. A few 16mm cameras hold 200 feet of film, and many are designed to use 400-foot magazines. A *magazine* is a separate housing for the film which attaches to the camera. The magazine holds a 400-foot core of film, which runs for 11 minutes and is extremely popular for documentary sound shooting.

The daylight loading spool prevents the film from becoming exposed while being loaded. The film to be used with a 400-foot magazine comes on a small plastic core and is not protected from exposure to light. In order to load the film into a magazine, the film can and the magazine must be placed inside a changing bag. This is a light-insulated black bag with zippers for inserting the film and holes for the cameraman's arms so that he can load the film without exposing it to the light.

shutter

Just behind the lens and in front of the aperture is the shutter, a thin disc which rotates on its central axis. If the shutter is exactly half a circle (180°), each frame will be exposed for $1/_{48}$ of a second and then covered for $1/48$ of a second, this latter time being when the next frame is pulled into place. It would turn, in 16mm or 35mm, at 24 rotations per second. With a few cameras, the shape of the disc can be changed to greater or smaller than 180°. This would allow the cameraman to vary the exposure time. However, with most cameras, the exposure time is a factor only of the camera speed. For most cameras, this would be $1/50$ of a second at 24 fps. If the camera speed were to be increased to 48 fps, the exposure time would be cut in half, or $1/100$ of a second.

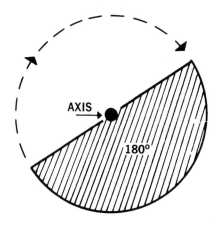

(*Fig.* 3) Frontal view of shutter operation

single-framing

Some cameras are also able to take single frames at a time. This is necessary for shooting animation (see chapter 9). There are also cameras, both in 16mm and 35mm, made especially for shooting animation.

projector

A projector operates on exactly the same principle of intermittent motion, film transport and shutter, the only difference being that the projector has a very bright light behind the film throwing the image onto the screen. It is this phenomenon that causes us to say that we spend thirty minutes in total blackness watching an hour film.

viewfinder

Most good cameras, including everything presently in the Super 8 line, have reflex viewfinders, which means that you see in the eyepiece exactly what is recorded on the film. This is so because the eyepiece and the film are fed images by the same lens.

Before the innovation of reflex viewing, cameras came with a separate lens for the viewfinder. This system is easier to make and therefore cheaper, but not as good, because picture framing was never exact. Even allowing for adjustment on such cameras, *parallax error* can never be completely eliminated. If two lenses are placed side by side and pointed in the same direction, the image that they "see," or *field of vision*, will be slightly different because of their different positions. If the lens for the eyepiece is adjusted so that its angle of vision intersects the lens's at the point of the subject, the background and foreground will, nonetheless, be slightly different. In Figure 4, note how correction of the foreground subject will automatically throw off the background. In the eyepiece we think we are framing both the foreground figure and the background house, but the processed picture will show the house with its roof cut off.

In a reflex camera either the image is reflected off a mirror on the front surface of the shutter, or part of the light coming through the lens is diverted away from the film to the eyepiece. Figure 5 is a diagram showing how light is reflected from a mirrored front surface of the shutter.

In this case, when the shutter is open, all the light

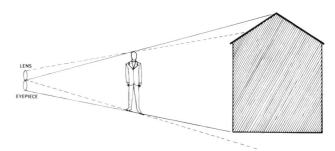

(*Fig.* 4) Example of parallax error

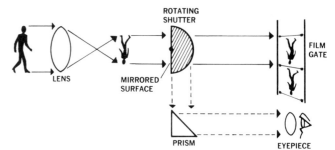

(*Fig.* 5) Reflex camera viewing system—intermittent image

goes to the film; when it is closed, all the light goes to the eyepiece. The advantage of this system is that no light is lost, either to the film or viewfinder. The major disadvantage is that at the end of a shot, the shutter is very often left in an open position. This means the cameraman is left in the dark, which can hamper his work, particularly in a documentary situation. Valuable time is lost while he manually adjusts the shutter to the closed position in order to frame his next shot.

The second reflex system in use (see Fig. 6) diverts some of the light at all times from the film to the viewer by use of a prism. Its major advantage is that the viewer is independent of camera operation, but its disadvantage is that 10-20% of the light is lost to the film.

One great advantage of the reflex viewfinder is that since you see exactly what the film "sees," whatever is in focus in the eyepiece will be in focus on the film.

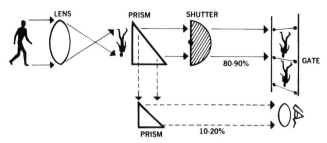

(*Fig.* 6) Reflex camera viewing system—split image

lens mount

Camera lenses, which will be detailed in the next chapter, are detachable from the camera body. The socket in the camera which holds the lens is called the lens mount. Camera lens mounts are either of a threaded, screw-in type or a bayonet type. This permits you to detach the lens and inspect the camera aperture any time after the film has been loaded without opening up the camera. Some cameras have a lens turret, which rotates so that more than one lens can be mounted on the camera and used for different shots.

filter slot

Just in front of the camera aperture, some cameras have a filter slot. This provision permits the insertion of a thin gelatin filter directly in front of the film plane. If there is no filter slot, a glass filter may be mounted in front of the lens when needed (see chapter 6). Super 8 cameras have built-in conversion filters for shooting interior film in daylight. When shooting indoors with lights, these filters are retracted by the operation of a key or switch.

camera noise

The simplest cameras make a certain amount of noise and cannot be used while recording sound because the microphone would pick up the camera noise. If a camera is noisy but must be used for a sound sequence, it may be covered by either a lightweight down comforter (commonly called a "barney") or a metal sound baffle (or "blimp") to deaden camera sound. Cameras specifically designed to be used while recording sound are made to operate as quietly as possible and are called silent, self-blimped or sound cameras.

motors and power

While some less expensive 16mm cameras are driven by a spring and are hand-wound, and some

(*Photo* 16) The Arriflex S camera with a 400-foot magazine and a 12-120mm zoom lens mounted on a tripod. The coiled power cable runs from back of camera to battery belt hung on front leg of tripod.

professional cameras may be driven by 110- or 220-volt house-current AC motors, most 16mm and all Super 8mm cameras have motors that are battery-driven. Some professional cameras have interchangeable motors and may be driven either by batteries or house current.

The advantage of a spring-wound motor is that you have neither the weight nor the frailties of batteries to cope with. Arctic cold, jungle humidity and heat, or lack of power to recharge are of no consequence. The disadvantages are the limited duration of the shot (20-30 seconds), the bother of winding and the lack of sound-shooting capacity. Nonetheless, many good films have been made on spring-wound 16mm cameras.

With a camera driven by an electric motor, you can press the start button and run through your entire load of film. This may be important in a long dramatic take or in a documentary situation, where the action won't stop for you to wind up again. There is also no valuable time lost between shots. A spring-driven motor runs more reliably in extreme cold weather, but since you probably won't be shooting in the Arctic, this is not a practical consideration.

All Super 8 cameras are driven by batteries housed somewhere in the camera, usually in the handle. Nickel-cadmium rechargeable batteries are standard for professional 16mm cameras and are recharged after each day's shooting by being plugged into either 110- or 220-volt house current. Weighing only a few pounds, they insure portability, and can either be strapped to your belt or carried in a separate battery case.

Spring-wound motors operate at variable speeds, usually from 8 fps to 64 fps, whereas battery-driven motors for 16mm cameras may be used either at constant speed, i.e., fixed for precisely 24 fps, or at variable speed. A constant-speed motor is governor controlled and is used when shooting with sound.

The governor is a device which regulates the speed of the motor so that it does not vary from the 24 fps needed for shooting with sound. As a battery is used throughout the course of a day, its voltage will drop. This will cause the speed of a variable-speed motor to drop, but not one that is governor controlled.

Variable speed or "wild" motors are generally used for shooting without sound and shooting for effect, that is, for slow and fast motion.

When shooting with sound, 16mm cameras can also be run from the house current by use of a "synchronous" motor. With these motors there are no batteries to worry about, and they use the 60-cycle pulse of the AC house current to regulate their speed at precisely 24 fps. These motors, as well as constant-speed motors, will be discussed again in greater detail in the chapter dealing with shooting with sound, or "sync" shooting.

Most Super 8 cameras range from about $50 to $500, with one or two that cost close to $1,000. The determining factors are the quality of the lenses and sync-sound capabilities. Cameras in 16mm range from the spring-wound (Bolex, Bell & Howell, etc.) at $500, to the precision Arriflex BL or Eclair at $10,000. A middle category includes the Beaulieu, Canon Scoopic, and Arriflex S, ranging from $1,000 to $3,000. Again, the choice of a zoom lens (see chapter 4) will increase the cost considerably. Cameras can, of course, be bought secondhand or rented.

summary

In this chapter we have seen that, in spite of the differences in viewing systems and motor drives, there is one central operation which is the basis for all motion-picture cameras: the intermittent movement of the film through the gate. The other basic function of the camera (which will be dealt with in the next chapter on lenses) is the formation of the image in the camera aperture at the front of the gate.

Although basic camera malfunction must be attended to by professionals, it is the camera aperture and the gate that require your periodic inspection. Remember, a piece of lint in the aperture will be magnified many times on the screen.

4. THE LENS: THE CAMERA'S EYE

---

focal length and angle of acceptance • wide-angle and telephoto lenses • setting the lens aperture: the iris and the f/stop • setting the focus: critical focus, depth of field • zoom lenses • lens care • lens shades

The camera lens has come a long way from the pinhole in Leonardo's "camera obscura." Film needs more light than a pinhole can yield; it needs light of uniform strength even though lighting conditions vary tremendously, and it needs an image precisely focused on the film plane. The camera lens meets all these needs. It has an adjustable opening, or aperture, which permits you to regulate the amount of light reaching the film plane, and a focusing ring which you can adjust to bring the subject into focus on the film plane.

Before considering the different kinds of camera lenses and what they do, it would be helpful to examine the function of the simple lens, a piece of optical glass with curved surfaces, which is the basic element of the camera lens.

Imagine a single point of light being reflected from your subject and falling on the film plane. This point is transmitted as a light ray which is a straight line. If it entered the camera through a pinhole, it would fall on only one point on the film plane and there would be no need to focus (Fig. 7A). But in order to be exposed at a fraction of a second, film needs more light than a pinhole can transmit.

If we make the hole larger in order to let in more light, the light rays from a point on the subject will then be permitted to fall over an area of the film plane (Fig. 7B). The point from the subject will no longer be represented as a point on the film plane, but as a diffused pattern which has no single point of focus. The function of the simple lens is, therefore, to collect the light rays and bring them to a point of focus on the film plane (Fig. 7C).

focal length and angle of acceptance

Camera lenses are referred to by their focal lengths. The greater the distance between the lens and the film plane (A-B in Fig. 10), the greater the focal length will be.

Focal length determines the angle of acceptance of a lens. The angle of acceptance, expressed in degrees, describes how wide a picture the lens sees. The human eye has a very wide angle of vision. Camera lenses normally have a much narrower span.

Figure 8 shows how the lens's angle of acceptance is greater the closer the lens is to the film plane, or the shorter its focal length. Lens A shows the subject from head to foot. Lens B is closer to the film plane and shows an area above and below

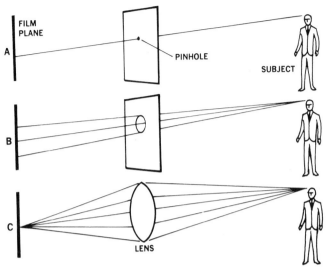

(*Fig.* 7) A, B and C demonstrate the principle of a simple lens.

(*Photo* 17) Typical series of five lenses for Arri S (counterclockwise from left): 12-120mm zoom, 10mm, 28mm, 50mm, 90mm macrolens

the subject. Lens C is further from the film plane and shows only part of the subject's face.

Lenses with short focal lengths have wide acceptance angles, while lenses with long focal lengths have narrow acceptance angles. Figure 8 gives a few examples of the relationship between focal length and the acceptance angle for standard 16mm lenses. For a quick reference to comparable 8mm lenses, divide the focal length by two, and for 35mm, multiply by two.

wide-angle and telephoto lenses

Lenses with short focal lengths are called wide-angle lenses, while lenses with long focal lengths are referred to as long, or telephoto, lenses. You will find the focal length of every lens, measured in either millimeters or inches, inscribed on the front of the lens housing.

In 16mm, a lens with a focal length of 25mm is called a normal lens. This is because the image it forms appears in normal perspective. That is, objects appear to have the same shape and size as they do in reality. A subject running toward the screen appears to be moving at the same speed that he would in reality.

Lenses which have a focal length of 15mm or less are usually referred to as wide-angle lenses. They have the quality of exaggerating the distance between objects and increasing the appearance of their depth and angularity. On the other hand, a lens with a focal length of 75mm is called a long lens, and has the opposite effect. It collapses the distances between objects and the camera, and flattens the object's angularity.

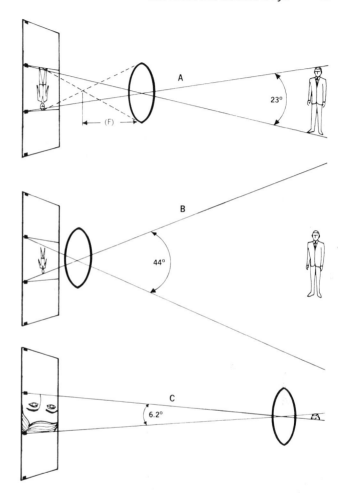

(*Fig.* 8) Lenses A, B and C show the relationship between the focal length (F) of a lens and its acceptance angle. A —25mm or normal-length lens; B—12.5mm, or wide-angle lens; C—100mm, or telephoto lens.

(*Photos* 18, 19, 20, 21) A series of shots keeping the subject-to-camera distance the same, but using lenses of different focal lengths: (upper left) 150mm telephoto;

(lower left) 75mm telephoto; (upper right) 25mm normal; (lower right) 15mm wide angle. Note that the range (from 15mm to 150mm) is equivalent to a zoom lens with a 10:1 zoom range.

(*Photos* 25, 26, 27, 28) Maintaining the same subject size by changing the subject-to-camera distance and using lenses of different focal lengths: (upper left) 15mm wide angle; (lower left) 25mm normal; (upper right) 75mm telephoto; (lower right) 150mm telephoto. Note the different scope of the background, the distortion of features by the wide-angle lens, and the glamorizing effect of the telephoto.

With a wide-angle lens, a figure running toward the camera appears to be covering a greater distance than he actually is. His speed of approach is exaggerated. A race photographed head-on with a long lens has the opposite effect; it will make the participants appear to be running at an even speed, since it de-emphasizes the distance between them. With a very long lens, they will appear to make little progress toward the camera. These are the lenses used to photograph horse races where, in spite of their strenuous efforts, the horses seem to get no closer.

A wide-angle lens may exaggerate the length of a nose, while long lenses are said to have a glamorizing effect.

Very long lenses, 100mm and up, are called telephoto lenses, and have the capacity to fill the screen with distant detail. The cameraman resorts to these lenses when he cannot move closer to his subject—for instance, in nature photography where he must remain hidden in a blind spot many feet from his subject.

the iris and the *f*/stop

We mentioned earlier that a lens must have an opening, or aperture, that is variable in size to compensate for changing light conditions. When we go into a darkened movie theater, our pupils

(*Photos* 22, 23, 24) The distorting effects of the wide-angle and telephoto lenses. The tendency of a wide-angle lens is to exaggerate distance: close objects look large, distant objects look farther away. The tendency of a telephoto lens is to compress distance. The center and bottom pictures were taken from the same spot.

dilate to admit more light, and when we come out, they contract in order to adjust to the strength of light that the retina receives. The iris is to the lens what the pupil is to the eye.

Film emulsion is even more sensitive than the retina to changes in light strength. It must receive a given strength of light at all times in order to yield shots with even brightness or density. In order for the lens to transmit this given strength of light, it is equipped with an iris which is similar in function to the iris of the eye. It is constructed of overlapping metal petals that expand and contract to change the aperture of the lens. This adjustment is measured by numbers known as *f*/stops, which are inscribed on the lens housing by the adjustment ring. You will most likely find a series of numbers as follows: *f*/2, *f*/2.8, *f*/4, *f*/5.6, *f*/8, *f*/11, *f*/16, *f*/22.

There are two things to understand. First, the larger the number, the smaller the lens aperture, or opening, will be. Thus, *f*/2 admits the most light and *f*/22 the least. This is because the *f*/stop number is calculated by dividing the focal length of the lens by the diameter of the iris opening. Using a 25mm, or normal lens, and opening the iris to the *f*/2 setting will give you an aperture diameter of 12.5mm, using the equation:

$$\frac{\text{focal length}}{\text{aperture diam.}} = f/\text{stop, or } \frac{25}{12.5} = f/2.$$

If the iris of the same lens is closed down to *f*/4, then the diameter of the aperture will be 6.25mm. Second, the interval between these numbers represents one *f*/stop.

A difference of one *f*/stop means that the light is either halved or doubled, depending on whether you are decreasing or increasing the aperture. For example, when you move the adjustment ring from *f*/5.6 to *f*/4, you have doubled the amount of light

f/2.8   *f*⅚   *f*/11

(*Fig.* 9) Various iris openings

reaching the film, and we say that you have "opened up" the lens. When you move from f/5.6 to f/8, you have halved the amount of light, and we say that you have "closed down" or "stopped down" the lens. The widest opening of a lens is known as its speed.

If a lens opens to f/1.4, a wider maximum aperture than most lenses have, we say that it is a fast lens and that its speed is f/1.4. Wide-angle lenses are generally faster than telephoto lenses because telephoto lenses require larger elements and are more difficult to construct. Fast lenses are useful because they allow you to work in more varied lighting conditions and, in particular, where the level of the light is low. Unfortunately, the faster the lens, the more expensive it will be.

setting the focus

The other adjustment ring on the lens housing controls focus. Since your subject will be at different distances from the camera, the camera lens must be adjusted so that it will be in focus on the subject and not some object which is in front of or behind it.

By the adjustment ring on the lens housing, there will be a series of numbers, often both in feet and meters, which correspond to the distance between the camera and objects at varying distances. One way to focus is by setting the indicator on the focusing ring opposite the number which represents the distance between your subject and the camera.

With a reflex viewing system, a better way to focus is by opening the lens to its widest aperture and, looking through the viewer, turning the focusing ring from one extreme to the other. As you go through the point of critical focus, the point which corresponds exactly to the distance between the subject and the camera, the subject will at first look soft, then increasingly sharp and soft again. Turn the ring back to the point where the subject looked sharpest. You are now in focus. If you usually wear eyeglasses, you will want to wear them while shooting to obtain the sharpest focus.

Focus is more critical for close-up objects than for distant ones. If you do not have a reflex viewing system, you will have to measure the distance of objects close to the camera, though objects at a distance may be estimated.

Once you have focused on your subject using the reflex viewfinder, look at the objects in front and in back of your subject. Objects in the foreground and background will look increasingly less sharp the farther they are from the subject. There is, however, an area in front and in back of your subject where all objects look acceptably sharp in detail. This is known as the depth of field.

depth of field

How great will the depth of field be, or how far in back and in front of your subject will objects appear to be in sharp focus? The answer to this depends on three factors. (See Fig. 10.) The depth of field will increase the higher the f/stop—or, again, the smaller the aperture. Second, at any given f/stop, the depth of field will be greater the shorter the focal length of the lens. Third—and the most basic consideration of all—the farther the camera (or, more precisely, the film plane) from the subject (A-C), the greater the depth of field will be.

As long as you are focused on your subject, why should you be worried about the depth of field?

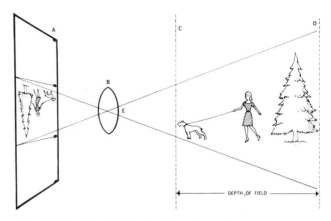

(*Fig.* 10) Depth of field: A—film plane; B—lens; C to D—depth of field; E—aperture. Everything between C and D is in focus.

Your area of interest may be split between foreground and background, and both must be in sharp focus. Take, for example, two figures confronting each other some distance apart in a long room. If the shot were to frame the length of the room and both subjects were to appear in sharp focus, you would have to consider the three factors listed above to solve your problem.

Let's begin with the simplest solution. You could move the camera far back from both subjects and shoot them with a long lens. But, as noted before, a long lens will give an image which will collapse the distance between the two subjects. This would distort the size of the room and might spoil a dramatic effect. Also, when shooting an interior, the cameraman may simply not be able to locate himself far enough back.

Taking the opposite tack, you might use a wide-angle lens for increased depth of field. But, as we have already seen, a wide-angle lens would distort the features of the figure in the foreground, and the exaggerated distance between the two subjects would cause the figure in the background to look very small.

The last option would be to use a normal lens and close down the aperture by using a higher f/stop. However, if you close down the lens opening, you will have to compensate by increasing the interior or studio light. This is what Orson Welles did for his deep-focus effects in *Citizen Kane*.

A common situation is to have an outdoor subject in the foreground close to the camera and, in the background, a beautiful panorama which you also want to be in sharp focus. Again, you must consider the three factors which will increase depth of field: using a higher f/stop, thus decreasing the opening of the lens; using a lens with a shorter focal length; and, lastly, increasing the subject-to-camera distance. In this case, there

(*Photos* 29, 30) Main subject size is the same in both pictures. Normal lens at top puts secondary subject in a relationship with the main subject and background. Telephoto lens (bottom) brings secondary subject closer, almost eliminating background, and has a much narrower depth of field.

would be nothing you could do about increasing the light.

Suppose that, instead of a panorama for a background, you have a busy street scene which distracts from the subject in the foreground. This is a case where you will want a narrow depth of field so that the background will appear in soft focus. The filmmaker chooses his lens on the basis of what he wants the audience to see. Long lenses with narrow depth of field are particularly good for picking a face out of a crowd.

What if you are using a normal lens, for example; how then can you decrease the depth of field without resorting to a longer lens? You can open up the aperture and shoot at a lower f/stop setting.

When we closed down the lens in order to increase the depth of field, we had to increase the strength of the lighting in order that the light reaching the film remained constant. Likewise, when you open up the lens, you must decrease the strength of the lighting. Of course, if you are outside, it will not be possible to affect the amount of lighting. In this case, you can use a neutral density filter to cut down the amount of light entering the lens (see chapter 6).

Lenses, like light bulbs, are either screwed into the camera or are inserted into a bayonet-type mount. If the lens is of the screw-in type, called a C-mount lens in 16mm, screw it securely into the mount, but never use force to tighten it. A bayonet-type lens is superior in this respect, since it cannot be tightened too much or too little or jammed into the mount.

zoom lenses

So far we have been discussing lenses which have a fixed focal length. A zoom lens, with which a Super 8 camera will most likely come equipped, answers the dream of varying the focal length without having to change the lens. The lens can be changed from close-up to wide-angle by simply turning an adjustment ring on the lens housing. This adjustment can be made while filming and stopped at any point within the zoom range.

As soon as you pick up a camera with a zoom lens, you will see that this is a great aid in framing and composition. For the documentary cameraman who must follow spontaneous and uncontrolled action, it is almost a necessity.

Many Super 8 cameras have built-in power zooms, that is, a zoom lens that is operated electrically. Zoom lenses on 16mm cameras are usually operated by a small hand-crank on the side of the lens. Whether regulated by hand or motor, the adjustment gradually increases or decreases the focal length of the lens. Increasing the focal length is called "zooming in," and the effect in the viewfinder is that the subject appears to come closer to the camera. Decreasing the focal length is called "zooming out," and the effect is that the camera appears to draw away from the subject.

Granted a zoom lens offers much, but are there any drawbacks? Zoom lenses are more complex in construction and have many more moving elements than a fixed focal-length lens to be kept in alignment for the best performance of the lens. Heat and bumps or jarring can cause any lens to go

Photos 31, 32) Busy background (left) is distracting. Background is made much less intrusive (right) by use of telephoto lens.

out of alignment and this presents a greater risk with the more fragile zoom lens.

Zoom lenses are generally not as fast as fixed focal-length lenses; that is, they generally transmit less maximum light. The lens combines, and is limited by, the features of the various focal lengths and, therefore, its speed is limited by the design problems created by the longer focal lengths. In addition, more light is lost in transmission through the lens because of the additional elements.

Super 8 zoom lenses are relatively fast due to the facility of constructing lenses with the smaller 8mm elements, as well as less extensive zoom ranges [the most popular 16mm zoom lens has a range of 12 to 120mm (10:1), while the average Super 8 zoom has a range of 12 to 36mm (3:1)]. In fact, Kodak has recently introduced a Super 8 camera with a zoom lens that has a speed of $f/1.2$, which is very fast.

The final comparison between the zoom and fixed focal-length lens has to do with image sharpness. The best fixed focal-length lenses are sharper than the best zoom lenses. The importance of this difference depends on the over-all standards of each gauge. In Super 8 cinematography, zoom lenses are standard. In 16mm professional work, a good zoom lens is generally acceptable, though, where detail is critical, a good fixed focal-length lens is preferred. Only in 35mm photography is the zoom lens usually restricted to the special effect of "zooming" as a camera movement.

An important point should be made about the way in which zoom lenses are focused. Reflex viewing allows adjustment of the focusing ring while looking at the subject through the lens. When using a zoom lens, focus in this way with the zoom at the end of its telephoto range; that is, where a subject close to the camera appears largest. Here, depth of field will be the least. Then, without

(*Photo* 33) Angenieux 12-120mm zoom lens. Turning hand-crank in center changes the focal length, either bringing subject closer (telephoto), or further away (wide angle). Numbers near crank show focal length. Numbers to left (toward front of lens) show focus, both in feet and meters. Numbers to right (toward back of lens) show $f/$stop. Note bayonet mount on back of lens.

changing focus, zoom back to the focal length you have chosen for your shot. If you decide to zoom in on that same subject while shooting, your shot will remain in focus.

lens care

There are some simple rules about lens care. Always replace the lens cap when the camera is not in use. This will protect the front element against accidental handling and scratching. Specks of dust on the front of the lens are inevitable and will not affect image quality. If dust particles are heavy and must be removed, blow them off or use a special camel's hair brush. Do not try to wipe dust off with a lens tissue. This will only scratch the lens as well as rub off the lens coating.

If you get a fingerprint or smear on the front element, this will affect image quality. First clean off the loose dust, as noted above, then apply a small amount of lens cleaning fluid or the moisture from your breath, and remove the smudge with delicate, circular movements, using *lintless* lens tissue.

lens shades

If the lens has a shade, use it. The shade blocks out light coming from outside the viewing perspective which can affect image sharpness by bouncing around inside the lens and, if it is strong enough, cause image flare. It also will protect the front of the lens.

summary

The function of the lens is to collect light rays and bring them to a point of focus on the film plane. Lenses are identified by their focal lengths, which tells you their acceptance angle, or viewing perspective, and their speed, which is their largest aperture given in *f*/stops. Lenses of variable focal length are called zoom lenses.

The *f*/stop is one of the adjustments you must make on the lens: this varies the amount of light transmitted by the lens to the film plane. The other adjustment is to focus. Depth of field refers to the distance in front and in back of your principal subject which appears acceptably sharp in focus.

5. FILM STOCK: ITS CHARACTERISTICS AND PROCESSING

speed • grain • latitude and contrast • black-and-white vs. color • super 8 cartridges • 16mm stock • dealing with the lab • projecting the work print

We have already learned that film consists of a celluloid base covered with a layer of light-sensitive emulsion. A point worth making is that celluloid, or more precisely, cellulose acetate, is not flammable. In the early days of motion pictures, a nitrate base which was very flammable and highly dangerous was used. Today this problem need not concern us.

Next we learned that the edge of the film bears perforations, or sprocket holes, which lock the film in the transport of the camera or projector, and which the pull-down claw engages in order to pull the next frame into place. Now it is time to discuss the characteristics of the emulsion itself and see how choices are made among the different film stocks available to us.

speed

Unexposed film is called raw stock. It has certain qualities and limitations that we should know about in advance. One of the most important features to know about the film is its speed. In the chapter on lenses, it was stated that the emulsion needs a certain amount of light to produce an image of medium brightness or density. The amount of light it needs defines its speed, which is in turn referred to by a number known as its ASA rating.

Let us consider two stocks, one rated at ASA 25 and the other at ASA 100. First, the higher rating indicates the faster film, or the film which needs less light to form an image. How much faster is the second film than the first? How does the ASA scale work? The stock with the ASA 25 rating is considered to be a slow film. In order to calculate the ASA rating of a film twice as fast, double the ASA number; i.e., twice 25 is 50. A stock with an ASA rating of 50 is considered a medium-speed film. That it is twice as fast as the first stock means that it needs half the amount of light to expose the same image. The lens would be set one f/stop higher than with the slower film.

Similarly, a film twice as fast as the medium-speed film would have an ASA rating of 100. This would be considered a fast film. Again, the lens would be set one f/stop higher than with the medium-speed film for the same shot, since half the amount of light is needed to expose the image properly. The film with the ASA 100 rating requires two f/stops less light for the same exposure as compared with a film with an ASA rating of 25. It needs one-fourth the amount of light for the same exposure.

What does this mean in terms of shooting? Let's assume that you are shooting a scene at *f*/5.6 with a film rated at ASA 25. The sun goes behind dense cloud cover and your light meter (covered in the next chapter) tells you that you must open up your lens to *f*/2. But suppose the widest opening on your lens is *f*/2.8. You'll need twice as much light as your lens will give.

If you had been using a stock rated at ASA 50, the film would have required half as much light as the film rated at ASA 25, and you could have shot the scene at *f*/2.8. With a film rated at ASA 100, you could have shot the same overcast scene at *f*/4. Doubling the ASA rating gives you an additional *f*/stop to work with, or, in other words, enables you to work with less light.

grain

Grain is associated with the speed of a film. Every film stock has a grain which is formed by the tiny dots of light-sensitive material which make up the emulsion. In still photography, the grain of an emulsion is often brought out in development to give the finished picture a certain texture. However, in motion pictures, because the grain pattern of each successive frame is not identical, the pleasing texture used in still photography is replaced by a swimming motion of tiny dots which is distracting, even irritating, on the screen.

The major problem in using high-speed emulsions has been that their grain is unacceptably apparent. In general, slower speed films have finer grain, medium-speed films have a medium grain, and high-speed films have the most grain. For greatest definition and least grain, always use the slowest speed emulsion possible under existing light conditions.

Measuring the intensity of the light and relating it to film speed and lens aperture will be the subject of the next chapter.

latitude and contrast

The third major characteristic of film stock is called latitude. If we look at an exposed frame of film, the extremes of its density are seen as black, which shows on the screen as darkness without texture, and clear film which shows on the screen as bright white without texture. Between these extremes of dark and light are all the shades of color that reveal the texture or character of the image. The range of shading on your subject that a film stock is capable of reproducing depends on its latitude.

Suppose your subject is standing in deep shade with a background of bright sunlight. Looking through the viewfinder, we can see clearly all the features on the subject's face as well as the colors of the flowers in the sunlit background and the texture of the dark earth in the deep shadow under the tree. The light may be eight times as bright in the sunlight and yet our eye loses nothing in detail. Assuming that we have set the lens aperture, or f/stop, for the light on the subject's face, what will the film record?

The regrettable answer is that the background will wash out; it will appear too brightly lit, lose its texture, and the dark earth in the deepest shade will appear as black. The latitude of the film does not encompass what we can see with our eyes. How we use film to record scene contrast so that it appears natural will be dealt with in the next chapter on exposure.

When a film stock reduces all light shades to white and all dark shades to black, we say that it has little latitude, and that its image appears "contrasty"—it produces too few shades of difference between dark and light.

black-and-white vs. color

There are two basic groups of film stocks—color and black-and-white—and two kinds of film in each group, negative and reversal. With reversal film, the image appears as the object would in reality. Negative film reverses the polarity of the image; that is, light areas appear dark and dark areas light. Despite its continued popularity in the field of still photography, there is little use of black-and-white film in today's motion picture industry. At this writing, approximately thirteen times as much color film is shot in 16 and 35mm as black-and-white. In Super 8mm, almost everything is shot and processed in color. Black-and-white represents an abstraction of reality, and its use is therefore based increasingly on an artistic rather than economic choice. Advocates of black-and-white film note its starkness and "documentary" quality.

Color film not only gives a more naturalistic portrayal of reality, but has the distinct advantage of communicating more information since different colors of the same intensity are recorded by black-and-white film as the same tone. It is easier to identify unfamiliar objects and background material on color film.

On the other hand, black-and-white film is generally cheaper than color film and, for this reason, is sometimes used for instruction in filmmaking classes and for low-budget documentary work.

super 8 cartridges

For Super 8 work, there are two different Eastman Kodak color stocks readily available in cartridge form. Kodachrome II costs a little more than $3.00* for a cartridge (50 feet) running over three minutes, and is rated at ASA 40 for artificial light and ASA 25 for daylight.

The second film stock is a recent development of fast-emulsion technology. Ektachrome 160 costs about $4.00 a 50-foot cartridge, which also runs for about three minutes, and is rated at ASA 160 for artificial light and ASA 100 for daylight. This is a high-speed film, and is all the more attractive since its grain is almost as fine as that of Kodachrome II.

Processing or development of either film stock costs about $2.50 a cartridge. Both are reversal films, which means they yield a positive or "real" image meant for direct projection.

Kodak also offers two black-and-white reversal films which are also available in cartridge form. Plus-X and Tri-X are respectively rated as slightly faster than the two color stocks already mentioned. They are not usually stocked by Kodak dealers, so you will have to hunt for them. Neither will Kodak process Super 8 black-and-white, so this will give you the additional problem of finding a lab that will. Kodak does not list the prices for these films, but they are usually more expensive to buy and process than color.

You may have noticed that the ASA ratings given above were given for both tungsten, or artificial

---

*All prices given in this chapter are subject to change and differences among laboratory processing fees are given only as a general guide.

indoor light, and for daylight. A color film emulsion is "balanced" (this will be discussed in the next chapter) for either artificial light or daylight. When an indoor film is used outdoors, the daylight must pass through a conversion filter before it reaches the emulsion. Some light intensity is lost when it is converted by the filter. This loss is reflected in the ASA ratings, so that you won't have to take the filter into account each time you measure the light. (Chapter 6 will detail the treatment and measurement of light.)

Color films are usually balanced for tungsten light and filtered in daylight situations since this conversion results in less loss of light than converting a daylight-type film for shooting with tungsten lights. Also, there is generally more daylight available, and the lower ASA rating when shooting in sunlight presents no problem.

16mm film stock

If you are preparing to work in 16mm, Kodachrome II is a stock geared for direct projection after processing. It is a quirk of the industry that Ektachrome 160 has not yet become available in 16mm. However, two other 16mm high-speed stocks are at your disposal: EF 7241, balanced for daylight with an ASA rating of 160; and EF 7242, balanced for tungsten with an ASA rating of 125. If 7242 is converted for daylight use, it is rated at ASA 80.

As with Kodachrome II, the EF stocks are designed for direct projection, though they have considerably more grain due to their higher speeds.

In black-and-white film, Kodak Plus-X Reversal (ASA rating 50 daylight/40 tungsten) and Kodak Tri-X Reversal (ASA rating 200 daylight/160 tungsten) are also available for direct projection. Think of Plus-X as comparable to Kodachrome, and Tri-X to EF, in both latitude and grain.

In beginning workshop situations, it is simpler and cheaper to edit (chapter 10) your processed camera original, the film originally exposed in the camera, and project the results without going through a work print, or copy, of the original. The color stocks so far discussed are not designed for duplication.

Professional work in 16mm is done with camera original which is not meant for direct projection but is designed specifically to be duplicated. There are no such stocks available in Super 8. When film is copied, the grain pattern is duplicated and becomes more apparent, the image more ''contrasty'' and the colors more harsh. If you duplicate a stock designed for direct projection, you will find the results unpleasant.

Professional stocks are designed with the notion that many prints will ultimately be made from the camera original for release and distribution. They are, therefore, fine-grain and low in contrast. The emulsions are soft, easily scratched and not meant to be projected.

When the camera original of a professional film is processed, a copy is immediately made; it is this copy that gives the director and cameraman the first view of their work. Normally, the original does not leave the lab and is kept in a vault. The copy is called the work print, and it is with this copy that the editor makes his initial cuts and experiments. Only at the very end—when every cut is final—is the original removed from the lab and matched with the work print (chapter 12).

It should be noted that the EF stocks are primarily meant for news cameramen, and their work provides the one exception to the above professional procedure. Here, exposed raw stock is processed, screened, edited and sent to the news editor for projection directly onto television news programs all in a matter of hours.

Of the two available 16mm color stocks designed for duplication, one is reversal and the other is negative. Though both are fine-grain stocks, Ektachrome Commercial, the reversal stock, has the least grain. Negative film shows the image density in reversed polarity; in other words, bright tones appear dark and dark tones appear bright. Both must be printed before they can be projected.

The greatest drawback to negative stocks is that any dust picked up inadvertently in the lab will be duplicated as white specks on the screen. These are much more distracting than dust on reversal film, which shows up as black. This disadvantage, as well as others involved in release printing (chapter 12), has made the reversal stock, Ektachrome Commercial, ECO 7252, by far the most popular color stock in 16mm professional work, even though it has a considerably lower ASA rating (see chart on page 88).

In black-and-white film, the Kodak reversal stocks are suitable for duplication as well as direct projection. Eastman black-and-white negative stock is, of course, meant only for duplication. Black-and-white negative offers the advantage of greatly increased latitude over reversal film. This means you will be more successful shooting scenes with great contrast, such as sun and deep shade, using negative film.

When you order 16mm film, a 100-foot length will come on a daylight loading spool, which should be loaded into your camera in subdued light. You will be asked whether you want single- or double-perforated film. Double-perforated stock is usually preferred because it is easier to handle on the editing table, while "single-perf" stock is used for single-system sound shooting (chapter 8).

16mm film stocks:

	ASA day/tung.	Costs		
		Stock 100'	Process 100'	Work Print
Kodachrome II, color reversal	25 40	$9.70	$6.00/100'	———
EF 7241-42 color reversal	160 125	7.80	.077/ft	$.08-.10/ft
ECO 7252 color reversal	16 25	7.10	.057	.08-.10
Eastman Color negative 7254	64 100	8.13	.063	.09
Kodak Plus-X, b&w reversal 7276	50 40	4.60	varies between 3¢	.07-.10
Kodak Tri-X, b&w reversal 7878	200 160	4.60	& 6¢/ft with minimum charge	.07-.10
Eastman Plus-X, b&w negative 7231	80 64	3.85	of at least $5.00 depending on lab	.06

Processing is a simple matter when you are using any of the color stocks designed for direct projection, whether 16mm or Super 8 cartridge. Simply go to your closest Kodak dealer or, if one is not located near you, you can use their prepaid-processing mailing pouches. You can also go to any motion-picture lab that deals with Kodak or is licensed to process Kodak film. However, they will usually not be interested in your business unless you are ordering a work print.

dealing with the lab

If you are at a more advanced stage and wish to work with a work print from a camera original such as ECO 7252, you must deal with a motion-picture lab. The cost of a work print varies, generally within the limits given in the above chart, depending upon which lab you choose and the services they provide.

Exposed film from a day's shooting can be expected to vary to some degree in density or brightness from shot to shot, and in color rendition or balance (chapter 6) from scene to scene. These differences are usually not intentional, and are distracting in an edited sequence. At the work print stage, though, this is not too important, so most people order what is known as a "one-light work print," which means that your work print is printed on one printing light, with no compensation for the scene-to-scene differences. For a slight additional charge, labs will pay more attention to the color rendition and density, and give you a more even work print by using a combination of printing lights. However, for economy's sake and for a work print that will tell you more about your mistakes, a "one-light work print" is recommended. You will also be asked whether you want a "double- or single-perf" work print. Double-perf stock generally facilitates handling in the editing room (chapter 10).

In addition, you should ask that the edge numbers be "printed through." There are numbers on the edge of your camera original. When a copy is made, these numbers are duplicated on the work print to facilitate matching the original at the end of the editing process (chapter 12).

An additional service the lab can provide is to have your camera original "pushed" in processing. This means that the original is held longer in the developer which, in effect, increases the ASA rating. This can be helpful in a case where you were forced to shoot without sufficient light. Most of the above-mentioned stocks can be pushed one and even two f/stops in processing without great loss in quality. However, some deterioration in image

(*Photo* 34) Edge numbers on original

quality does occur. With reversal color stocks, the grain becomes more apparent and the darker colors tend to lose their density. There will also be an extra charge for this service.

projecting the work print

When you pick up your work print and are about to thread it on a projector, which way should the film be wound as it comes off the reel? Should the emulsion be on the inside or on the outside? When you load a spool of film into your camera, you will notice that the emulsion is on the inside as it comes off the spool, so that it will face the lens. It *must* face the lens to be exposed. This is called camera wind, or B-wind (*wind* from *winding*).

When the original is duplicated at the lab, it goes through a process called contact printing. The emulsion of the original "contacts" the emulsion of the work print, with the result that the emulsion is on the opposite side of the base on the work print. This is called A-wind, or printing wind. Therefore, when you thread your work print on the projector, the emulsion should face *away* from the lens, the opposite of the way you would treat the camera original which, if projected, would have its emulsion, or dull side, facing toward the lens so that left to right appear as left to right on the screen. If you are working without a work print, with reversal stock, then the emulsion side would always face the lens, the same as it would in the camera.

Super 8 film is generally returned from the lab on a small spool ready for projection. On the other hand, 16mm film is usually returned wound on a small plastic core and must be transferred to a reel for projection. A split reel, which will unscrew at

(*Photo* 35) The split reel opens by unscrewing, permitting the handling of film on cores.

the center, divide into two halves and accept the plastic core, will save much time and effort in rewinding. Once on a reel, the film is threaded automatically on the projector with almost all Super 8 units and with 16mm projectors of recent design. A standard older projector is the Filmosound, which is threaded manually. You will find a threading diagram on the projector and will have no problem if you remember that the loops must be large enough to allow the intermittent movement at the gate, just as in the camera (see photo 36).

summary

In general, in the workshop situation, you will be working with color reversal stock designed for direct projection. When using this kind of stock, you will deal directly with Kodak for processing, either through a dealer or by mail. If you are at a more advanced stage, you will use a camera original, which is designed specifically for duplication and is not meant to be projected. To see your work, you must order a work print. You will have to deal with a lab which is equipped for this purpose, and give them an order with certain specifics; e.g., a one-light work print on double-perf stock with edge numbers printed through. When you get your work print and thread it on the projector, the emulsion should face away from the lens, toward the bulb, in order for left to right to appear as left to right on the screen. If you are not using a work print, the emulsion should face toward the lens as it must in the camera.

(*Photo* 36) Bell & Howell 16mm projector in front of projection window. White leader is threaded to show path of film from top feed reel to back take-up reel.

(*Photo* 37) The Bolex Super 8 automatic-threading projector. Most Super 8 projectors have automatic-threading devices.

(*Photos* 38, 39, 40) (From top to bottom): underexposed, overexposed, correctly exposed

6. LIGHT: ITS MEASURE-MENT, CONTROL AND CREATION

reflected and incident light reading • scene contrast • built-in exposure systems • hand-held exposure meters • filters • color balance • lighting • soft and hard light • night effects

Now that we have chosen a shooting stock, we know its speed, or sensitivity to light. This is constant. We will find our subject, however, in everything from low-level interior light and dark shade to the brightest daylight conditions of snow or sand. Lighting conditions vary widely from one situation to another. How do we relate these different strengths of light to the film's requirement of a constant amount of light? We measure the light and set the variable aperture on the lens. This is called setting the exposure.

If our measurement was correct, the results will show a normal exposure. When an incorrect measurement is made and too much light reaches the film, the result will be overexposure; if too little light reaches the film, underexposure.

There are two systems for measuring light: one is called a reflected light reading; the other, an incident light reading (Fig. 11). Both utilize a mechanical device called a light meter, or exposure meter (photo 41). To accurately measure reflected light, point the meter toward the subject from the direction of the camera. To measure incident light, put the meter where the subject would be and point it toward the camera. Most meters can be adjusted to read either reflected or incident light, but they are primarily designed for one or the other light-reading systems.

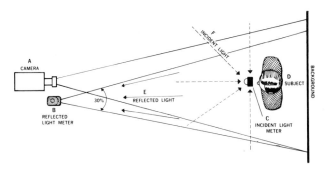

(*Fig.* 11) Incident and reflected light reading. A—camera; B—reflected light meter; C—incident light meter; D—subject; E—reflected light; F—incident light.

reflected light reading

The basic assumption of the reflected light-reading system is that each scene should have a balanced brightness and that each shot should have an overall medium density. In general, the reflected light meter is pointed toward the scene from the position of the camera. When a camera is equipped with an automatic exposure system, it has a reflected light meter which is actually inside the camera and sees the scene exactly as the lens sees it.

When the camera is not equipped with such a system, a hand-held meter is used. A hand-held reflected light meter reads the scene approximately as the lens sees it. A typical meter of this type reads the scene with a 30° acceptance angle. What the meter does is this: it reads the varying degrees of brightness of all the objects in the scene, and comes up with an average for the whole scene. The number it gives will tell you how to set the exposure so that the scene will have a medium density, or brightness, when projected onto the screen. This medium density is often called a medium grey for

(*Photo* 41) The two different kinds of light meters: (left) the Gossen Lunasix, used chiefly as a reflected meter (note window in center); (right) the Spectra Pro, used chiefly as an incident meter. Both meters will take either incident or reflected-light readings.

visual reference in discussing lighting calculations.

The system described above works well for the documentary cameraman who is most often in the position of trying to follow the general action in front of him. Let us suppose, however, that we are not interested in the over-all scene, but in a particular subject. What happens if we expose our subject for medium grey?

Few subjects represent medium grey. Some people are light-skinned, others are dark. Flesh tones will be scaled according to the degree of brightness of other objects in the scene, and if we take a general reflected light reading of the whole scene, the exposure will probably look realistic when projected on the screen. If, however, we take a close-up of the subject, we will be interested in only one value: the brightness of the subject's skin tone.

When taking a reflected light reading of a face for a close-up, the meter is pointed toward the face and held close to it. It tells us how to expose the face to look medium grey, or medium in density or brightness. However, this exposure will make a light-skinned face look too dark and a very dark face look too light. By experience we learn that we must compensate for this. Opening up the lens an additional *f*/stop is one way to get the right exposure for the average light-skinned face. Then when filmed and projected, that face will look not medium grey, but light-skinned.

There are other tricks that can be played on the reflected light meter. Suppose the subject is standing against a very dark background and we are taking a medium shot. The meter reading will be based mostly on the density of the very dark background. Again, it will indicate how to expose a medium grey. When we project the film, the background will look almost medium in brightness and the light-skinned subject will be overexposed.

If part of the scene is extremely bright, for example, back light from the sky or bright reflections of the sun off water, this small portion of the scene—but extremely intense source—will throw off the whole reading. The meter will calculate the bright reflections into the average and, in most cases, the scene will be underexposed. To obtain a truer rendition of this shot, point the meter away from the bright reflections, use that reading, then point the camera toward your original shot. The subject will then be properly exposed and the reflections will be extremely bright.

incident light reading

We have seen how the aim of the *reflected* light reading—particularly of the systems built into the camera—is to give an exposure of medium density, or medium grey, to each scene. The aim of *incident* light reading is to give uniform skin tones from scene to scene and from shot to shot within the scene. Take, for example, a sequence in which we move from a medium shot of the subject to a close-up of the face. As was previously seen with our light-skinned subject, a reflected light reading of the skin tone alone will give us a close-up in which this tone is darker than it would appear in the medium shot.

With an incident light reading, the meter is held next to the subject and is pointed toward the camera to measure the intensity of the light falling on the subject. The incident light meter measures the light falling on only one spot: the subject. It is not affected by the varying degrees of brightness of other objects in the scene.

The head of a reflected light meter is a small

(*Photos* 42, 43) Reflected light meter (top) is pointed at subject. Incident light meter (bottom) is placed near subject, facing camera.

aperture which admits the light. An incident light meter has a hemispherical head which looks like half a Ping-Pong ball and should always be pointed toward the camera.

The light which falls on the subject is called incident light, and it is this light that the meter measures. The reflected light meter, remember, measures light reflected by the subject, or the subject's brightness.

The difference between the two systems may be difficult to understand at first, and it bears repetition. When we used the reflected light meter for the close-up of our subject, it read the light reflected from the light skin tones, and registered a number which told us how to expose the face as medium grey. We were in trouble because we didn't have a medium-grey subject, and we had to make an adjustment to the given reading.

With the rounded head of the incident light meter pointed toward the camera and held next to the subject, we measure the intensity of the light falling on the subject. The meter is like a baseball glove "catching" the light rays coming toward the subject. We no longer measure facial tones which vary, but the constant light falling on one spot; therefore, we do not have to make any adjustments for different subjects who reflect light differently.

scene contrast

Incident light reading is linked to the highly critical standards of feature-film cinematography, where the star's face must appear the same from shot to shot and from sequence to sequence. This is not always our main concern, as we have previously noted with the documentary cameraman. He is usually interested in the evenness of the whole scene, rather than the skin tones of a particular subject. Let's go back to an earlier illustration when the concept of film latitude was being discussed.

Our subject was standing in deep shade underneath a tree with a background of flowers in bright sunshine. The background was eight times as bright as the area in the shade, and we found that the latitude of the film did not allow us to record the brightness range. The film could not record both the area of deep shade and the bright, sunlit background.

The latitude of color reversal film is slightly over four f/stops. For everything in a scene to reproduce with realistic texture, the difference between the lightest and the darkest object in the scene should not be more than four f/stops in order to fall within a safe margin of the film's latitude.

Suppose you take a reflected light reading of only the darkest object in the scene, and the light meter gives you a reading of f/2.8. Taking a reading of the brightest object in the scene gives you f/11. If you then shot the scene at f/5.6, halfway between f/2.8 and f/11, the lightest and the darkest objects in the scene would be at the limits of the film's latitude, and would retain some texture. Anything darker would reproduce as black without any texture at all. The texture of anything lighter would wash out.

How would you photograph the scene mentioned earlier with color reversal film? Suppose the deep shade in the foreground with the subject had a reading of f/2.8. Suppose the sunlit background had a reading of f/8. This would make an average difference of three f/stops. The difference between the brightest object in the sunshine and the darkest object in the shade would be much more. If you set the exposure at f/2.8 for a normal exposure of your

(*Photo* 44) If figures are in shade, proper exposure for skin tone may cause background, in sunlight, to wash out.

subject in the shade, the average object in the sunlit background would fall outside the reversal film's latitude, which would range roughly four stops from $f/1.4$ to $f/5.6$, or two stops above and below $f/2.8$. Even if you slightly underexposed the foreground and set the exposure for $f/4$, the brighter objects in the background would still be overexposed.

In an elaborate production, the solution would be to increase the brightness of the shade area by the use of sun reflectors or fill lights. Your solution would be to confine the shot entirely to the shade area or bring the subject out into the sun.

In another example, suppose the shade area around the subject were not deep shade—say $f/4$, and that the sunlit background were only two stops brighter; that is, the shade area is $f/4$ and the background is $f/8$. Then shooting the scene at $f/5.6$ would bring most of the objects in the scene within the film's latitude.

If you took a reflected light reading of the whole scene—foreground shade and background sunlight—which is what an automatic exposure system in the camera would do, how would the subject appear on the screen?

Because the meter would average out the background and shade area, the subject would appear darker than normal. But a face in the shade is indeed darker than in normal light, and in this context, the results would look realistic and be satisfactory for most purposes.

An incident light reading taken in the shade would make no attempt at balancing the whole scene, and would render skin tones as bright as they would have been if the subject were photographed in the sun. The difference in image contrast and the modeling of the light would tell you which shot had been made in the shade and which in the sun, but the brightness would be consistent.

(*Photos* 45, 46, 47) Filming a subject in front of a window allows several options. By exposing for the bright outdoors (top) the subject becomes a silhouette. By exposing for the interior subject (bottom) the exterior washes out. The center is a compromise.

In a close-up of the subject, this might appear satisfactory, but a shot of the entire scene would not be balanced. The facial tones would not give the feeling of shade, and part of the background would be overexposed.

Light reading of a professional standard is a complex subject. Working with the automatic exposure systems of Super 8 cameras, you will not be bothered initially by the above concerns, but as you go on, you will find more and more shots that somehow displease you. And if you become involved in 16mm work, your camera will probably not come equipped with an automatic exposure system, and you will have to learn to take independent light readings. There is no substitute for experience in finally getting the results you want.

built-in exposure systems

Exposure systems that are built into the camera are basically of two kinds. The first, the fully automatic system which you will probably find on your Super 8, reads the light, and a small motor drive automatically adjusts the lens aperture. An indicator in the viewfinder will tell you whether a dark scene is beyond the lens's capability. The exposure system is preset for the ASA ratings of the film cartridges the camera can accept. The camera's speed is also incorporated into the light reading. Most of these systems read from behind the lens, though some are designed around a separate aperture.

The second kind of system is semiautomatic. The correct f/stop is given in the viewfinder and you must manually adjust the aperture ring on the lens to that f/stop.

If the camera, such as a 16mm model, is not

(*Photos* 48, 49) The flat lighting of direct sunlight (top) causes the face to lose detail. The softer lighting of shade or overcast sky (bottom) creates three-dimensional contours.

cartridge-loading, then a separate adjustment must be made when you load the camera to incorporate the ASA rating of the film.

hand-held exposure meters

The simplest of the hand-held meters to operate is the Spectra incident light meter (photo no. 41). Initially, you insert a screen into the meter designed for the ASA rating of the film you are using; then the meter will read directly in *f*/stops. The reading indicated is based on the assumption of a 1/50th of a second shutter speed, which applies to most 16mm cameras running at 24 fps. An attachment permits the reading of reflected light.

The Gossen Lunasix meter (photo 41) is basically a reflected light meter, though a simple adjustment turns it into a fairly good incident meter. After you have set the meter for the proper ASA rating, you take a light reading. The reading gives you a number which you adjust on a scale, and then read off a frames-per-second scale against a scale of *f*/stops. For 16mm film, you can also read the *f*/stop opposite 1/50 second when shooting at 24 fps. Generally, you will read off against 24 fps, but note that when you are shooting a slow-motion effect, you will read, for example, 48 fps against the scale of *f*/stops.

With any meter, you must take into account three different factors to arrive at the correct exposure: first, the brightness of the scene, or the intensity of the incident light; second, the ASA rating of your film stock; third, the exposure time which is based on the frames-per-second speed of the camera.

(*Photos* 50, 51) Side lighting (top) accentuates modeling of faces and is much more pleasing than flat frontal lighting. Back lighting (bottom) separates subject from background.

filters

The most common use of a filter in color cinematography is to convert a tungsten-balanced film for daylight use. This will be the case, for instance, if you are using either Ektachrome Commercial or Eastman Color Negative for shooting stock. Neither of these stocks comes balanced for daylight, so a filter must be utilized when shooting outdoors. If you shoot an "indoor," or tungsten-balanced, film without a conversion filter outdoors, the resultant image will appear "cool," that is lacking in reds and strong in blues. And just the opposite will happen if you use a film balanced for daylight indoors with lights: the image will have no blues and will have a "warm" reddish-brown cast.

The eye does not discriminate between the "blue" light of daylight and the "red" light of incandescent lights, but color emulsion does. The function of the conversion filter is to emphasize that part of the color spectrum that is being lost. When you shoot an indoor film outdoors, you are losing reds, so the filter is reddish in color. Conversely, the filter for converting outdoor film is blue in color.

Much more light is lost by use of the blue filter than the reddish filter, so most professional stocks are balanced for tungsten and used with a #85 conversion filter when used in daylight where the light loss is more acceptable. When using a #85 conversion filter, the light loss is two-thirds of a stop. In order not to have to subtract two-thirds from the f/stop for every light reading, the ASA rating of the film is changed. For example, when using ECO 7252, rated at ASA 25 for tungsten light, the ASA scale on the meter is adjusted to ASA 16.

(*Photos* 52, 53) Same scene shot with (top) and without (bottom) polarizing filter. Note how polarizing filter separates sea and sky.

Another kind of filter which is commonly used is called a neutral density filter. As the name suggests, the filter does not affect the color balance; it is neutral toward color. It does cut down the amount of light reaching the lens. You may have to use a fast film in strong light, and the smallest aperture of the lens will not reduce the amount of light sufficiently. Or you may not want to use a lens at its smallest aperture. Most lenses do not give their sharpest image at the smaller apertures, and operate better in the mid-range of the f/stop scale.

Alternatively, you may not want the great depth of field that is produced by the smaller apertures, as is the case when you want a soft-focus background. In all these situations, you would have to cut down the light with a neutral density filter.

A third kind of filter is called a polarizing filter. This filter is used to obtain a deeper blue in the sky, increase the definition of distant objects or reduce distracting reflections of a shiny surface; for example, distracting reflections on a glass window. When a polarizing filter is used, there is less light reaching the film, and this is complicated by the fact that the loss of light depends on the angle between the sun, or source of light, and the camera. The loss is greatest when this is a right angle, as it is at noontime. Any camera movement must take this into consideration. However, despite this complication, beautiful scenic effects can be achieved with this type of filter.

There is a series of filters used in professional work called color-compensating filters. They can be used to correct the color balance of light under certain conditions so that a realistic color rendition is maintained. We have spoken of film stock being balanced for either daylight or artificial tungsten light. Both the "daylight" and "3200° K. tungsten" ratings that appear on the film package are norms which approximate real conditions. Compensating filters correct the differences from these norms. Shifts in color from skylight to candlelight are based on the difference of the color temperature of the light source, and this concept is essential to understanding not only the dynamics of this type of filter, but also to color photography and cinematography as well. The use of compensating filters, however, is a complex craft and is not advisable for beginning film production.

color balance

The visible spectrum is made up of the whole rainbow of colors, ranging from red to yellow, green, blue and violet. Different light sources are more intense in one part of this spectrum than another.

The way light affects color emulsion is determined by measuring the color temperature of the light source on a scale of Kelvin degrees. This rating tells you the proportion of red to blue emitted by the light source; that is, the sky or an incandescent light. Kelvin temperature ratings are easily understood on the basis of the simple relationship that the higher the number, the "bluer" the light will be; and, conversely, the lower the number, the "redder" the light will be.

Daylight is a mixture of sunlight and blue skylight. Average summer sunlight plus blue skylight is rated at 6500° Kelvin at high noon. A 100-watt household bulb is around 2800° Kelvin, and a candle flame is rated at 1850° Kelvin.

When shooting exteriors you will be faced with daylight which differs from the norm of approximately 6000° Kelvin for which your film is balanced. When the sun is not directly overhead, its color temperature is lowered. For example, one hour after sunrise the rating is 3500 degrees, while in late afternoon it is 4300 degrees. These conditions will cause your projected image to look reddish, since the color temperatures are lower than the norm.

Average summer shade, which is mostly illuminated by blue skylight, has a rating of 8000 degrees, and a scene shot in the shade will have a bluish cast when projected.

Avoid shooting during the first few hours after sunrise and late afternoon; otherwise, you will have to live with the reddish results or use the proper color-compensating filter. In 16mm work, less extreme variations can be corrected at the time of the final answer print (chapter 12).

The lights which you will use for lighting interiors are usually rated at 3200° Kelvin, the tungsten rating of your "indoor" color film stock. When you use lights with this rating, the results will be realistic and the color balance will appear true. The only problem you may confront in using these lights is where you have additional artificial light or window light in the room.

There is a simple solution for dealing with unrated incandescent light or fluorescent light that is in the same room with photographic lights. Turn it off, since it will deteriorate the color balance. Window light, which is actually daylight, can be similarly treated by pulling the shade.

If a window showing a daylight exterior must be in the shot, there are two basic solutions from which to choose. Either you must use filters for the lights to convert their color temperature to that of daylight, or cover the window with #85 gelatin sheets to convert the daylight to a 3200° tungsten temperature.

If you are lighting for black-and-white film, you will have no color-balance problems and can use any incandescent bulb, whatever its rating.

lighting

Lighting interiors can be one of the most creative aspects of motion-picture photography. In a compelling sense, it allows you to create your own reality. If you are sufficiently creative, you can have your subject in soft, oblique window light, or in flickering candlelight without ever revealing the source to the audience.

The lighting alone can set the mood for a scene. Long shadows and low-key lighting can give a room an ambiguous, mysterious quality. The swing of sharp headlights through the window of a darkened room can be alarming. Flat or even lighting creates a humdrum or businesslike atmosphere.

In designing your lighting, there are always two basic considerations: what is the source of the light in your mind's eye, and what is its quality. Once you have decided upon these two considerations, you can begin to mold the situation even with only a few lights at your disposal.

The quality of light on the subject has to do with the contrast it produces. Conventionally, lighting contrast is discussed in terms of the lighting ratio—the relationship of the key light plus the fill light to the fill light alone. The key light is the main, or strongest, light; the fill lights are the supplementary lights (Fig. 12). The angle of the key light indicates the position of the main light source in the screen image, or where the light appears to come from to the audience. Fill light is needed to supplement the key light in order to fill in shadows on the subject that would otherwise appear too harsh and distorting. Remember, color emulsion is much more sensitive to light contrasts than your eye.

(*Photos* 54, 55, 56, 57) Basic lighting techniques: (upper left) the key light alone; (lower left) the key light with fill light; (upper right) key light, fill light and back light; (lower right) flat lighting with a single light bounced off the ceiling.

The back light (Fig. 12) is used to outline the shape of the head and separate it from the background. This is a nice effect, though it does have a peculiar "studio light" quality.

Suppose the key light is twice as strong as the fill light. If we say that the fill light represents one unit of light and the key light two, then the lighting ratio would be three to one, or one plus two over one. according to the definition given above. This would mean there would be up to a one-and-a-half f/stop difference between the darker and lighter areas of the subject's face.

If we recall that the latitude of color film is approximately four f/stops from the lightest to the darkest object within the frame, it is clear that this difference in the skin tones alone will give the subject plenty of contrast. A lighting ratio of three to one generally should not be exceeded when working with color film unless a special effect is desired. Since color itself molds the object, an even lower lighting ratio is often satisfactory.

In exteriors where the subject is in bright sunlight from a clear sky, the shadow under his chin may well be several f/stops below the sunlight on his cheek, which would exceed the lighting ratio given above. In documentary photography, this high contrast is usually ignored and nothing is done to brighten shadow areas. A feature film, on the other hand, would normally require the use of fill lights or reflectors to lighten the shadow area. Since the latitude of black-and-white reversal film is comparable to that of color, the lighting considerations will be similar. However, with black-and-white negative stock, the lighting contrast can be considerably higher.

Because television electronics cannot accept high contrast, films made especially for TV have extremely flat lighting. Here the lighting ratio is only two to one. It is this uniform lack of contrast,

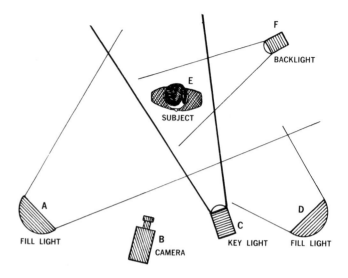

(*Fig.* 12) A basic lighting setup: A and D—fill lights; B—camera position; C—key light; E—subject's position; F—back light.

the absence of interesting shadows, that makes the TV image so flat and dull.

It is important to keep in mind the problems of continuity in lighting for shots that will be matched later in editing. Whether shooting in sunlight or artificial light, the direction and contrast of the light must be maintained; otherwise discontinuity will result. Where light cannot be controlled, as with changing sunlight, it may be necessary to reshoot the shot or shots that do not match.

soft and hard light

Lighting contrast is also affected by the quality of each individual source of light. We refer to a light as being either hard or soft, a description which has nothing to do with the intensity of the light, but with the effect that single light has on shadow lines. If it throws a sharp shadow line, we call it a hard light; if the shadow line is diffused and barely noticeable, we call it a soft light.

The more personal the film, the more natural and intimate the lighting should look, and the less an audience will tolerate the effect of studio lighting. Soft light gives a more natural rendering on color film, while most studio lights are harsh because of the small area of the light source. To make any light softer, there are several things we can do.

First, we can use a bounce light technique. If your interior has white walls or ceiling, you can bounce light off these surfaces. Photographic lights are extremely hot, and if a light is too close to a reflecting surface, it can scorch. Also, if the surface is not white, you will change the color balance of the light.

Another common procedure is to hang spun

glass in front of the light. This spreads the light source over many tiny reflecting surfaces. Another technique is to reflect the light off any rough, silvered surface, such as crinkled aluminum foil.

When planning the key light, always bear in mind the source of the light as it will appear in the screened image. If the light is supposed to be coming from the ceiling, angle the key light high. If it is coming from a table lamp or a window, angle the key light across from the subject. If you think things out realistically, your interior will not look like some anonymous space.

night effects

Night effects in interiors can easily be created—again keeping in mind the source of the light—by increasing the lighting contrast and, sometimes, by underexposing the shot. Exterior night effects can be achieved outside at night with artificial lights, though this quickly becomes quite complicated. An easier way of filming nighttime exteriors is called day-for-night filming.

Day-for-night is a technique whereby you film in daylight and underexpose from one-and-a-half to two f/stops to achieve a nighttime effect. The best effects result when the sun is to the side of or slightly behind the subject and the subject is shot against a dark background. Try to keep the sky out of the shot when you frame. The bluish cast of moonlight can be simulated by using interior, or tungsten-balanced, film and omitting the filter.

(*Photos* 58, 59, 60) Dramatic or night lighting (top): dramatically angled key source, little or no fill light, and underexposure. (Center) the same key light as in top photograph gives the appearance of a sun-splashed interior when fill light is added and the film is exposed normally. The face (bottom) is lifted out of the background by use of different zones of light.

lighting systems

The more lighting effects you devise, the more creative you will become, and you will find that you can be imaginative with an extremely simple lighting setup. There are a number of lightweight, portable lighting systems available for your use.

The Lowell lighting kits are relatively inexpensive and consist of a number of color-balanced, ioographic reflector bulbs, sockets and extension cords. These kits are useful for small, easily assembled lighting setups, such as the corner of a room that will be used for an interview. When more light is required, quartz lights are recommended.

The quartz light is a recent development of lighting technology. These small bulbs produce a tremendous amount of light and have a relatively long life. Differing from reflector bulbs, which use ordinary sockets, quartz bulbs require special housings. The Lowell and Colortran lighting systems are, nonetheless, portable and uncomplicated.

When selecting a quartz light, you should know whether you will require a fill or spot characteristic. Most of the quartz housings have a two-position adjustment; some are fully adjustable from fill to spot characteristics. A fill light throws a broad, even beam of light, while the beam of a spotlight is narrow and concentrated. Key lights generally have more of a spot characteristic. Other quartz lights are made specifically for a single function, such as lighting a large, flat area or throwing "soft" light.

Reflector bulbs and quartz lights can be powered by normal building circuits, but bear in mind that the average fuse for a circuit is set for a maximum of 15 amps. This means that you should not load any one circuit with more than 1500 watts of light.

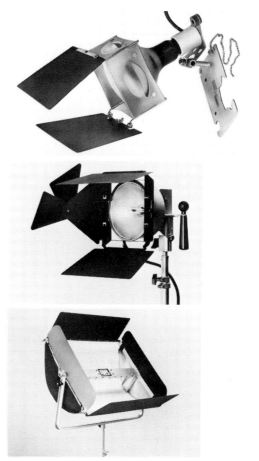

(*Photos* 61, 62, 63) Three Lowell lights: (top) a versatile lighting bracket which uses photographic reflector bulbs. The black flanges, or side panels, are called "barn doors" and are used to shape the throw of the light. (Center) A focusing quartz light. A lightweight housing and efficient quartz-iodine bulb combine to produce a portable, high-intensity light. (Bottom) A soft light. The concave reflector produces a soft, even source of light which affects modeling much like the light from an overcast sky.

summary

In setting the exposure, keep in mind three things: the ASA rating of your film; the exposure time, which is 1/50th of a second for most cameras when shooting at 24 fps; and the brightness of the scene or the intensity of the light falling onto the subject. A reflected light reading measures the brightness of a scene, and its goal is to achieve an even brightness, or medium density, from shot to shot. An incident light reading measures the intensity of the light falling on the subject, and its goal is to maintain constant skin tones. Most Super 8 cameras have automatic exposure systems which set the lens aperture by means of a behind-the-lens reflected light-reading system.

Every light source has its own color temperature which will affect the color balance of your shot. If you avoid early morning and late afternoon shooting and use a film balanced for daylight or a film balanced for tungsten light with a #85 conversion filter, your exterior colors will appear realistic. If you shoot an interior with film balanced for tungsten light, you should use lights rated at 3200° Kelvin, and turn off all fluorescent or other unrated lights.

When lighting an interior, you should be concerned primarily with two things: the source of the light in your mind's eye and the quality of the light. Both the lighting ratio and the character of each individual light, whether hard or soft, affect the quality of the lighting. The lighting ratio should generally be 3 to 1 or less when working with color film. The position of the key light determines the feeling of the source of light in the screened image. Once you have decided upon the source of light, you can experiment and be creative with a relatively simple lighting setup.

7. SHOOTING THE FILM: CREATING THE IMAGE

the flow of images: continuity of space, time and motion • continuity of an event: cutaways and reaction shots • parallel action • camera movement: pan, tilt, zoom, dolly, tracking and crane shots • vehicle speed vs. screen speed • following focus and completing the movement • tripod vs. hand-held shooting • composition and framing • setting up • shooting with sound • start mark • super 8 sync sound

Film is the flow of images. Creating that flow and making it compelling and clear is the craft of filmmaking. Before shooting a single shot, we must have an idea of what will come before and what will follow it. If we do not, chances are slim that a cohesive film will result in the editing room.

Sometimes this chance is calculated, as in documentary filmmaking where the editor can work with twenty to one-hundred times the footage that will finally be used in the film. This is considered a high shooting ratio. In your case, the ratio will be low; you will be using much of what you shoot. To do this successfully, your shots must be organized and balanced so that the final film will flow smoothly. In order not to distract and confuse the audience, your sequences of shots should appear unbroken and coherent. This quality is called continuity.

Film continuity (continuity of space, time and motion) has its own special rules. Let's look at a simple situation to see how they work. Take the old custard pie routine in slapstick comedy. Comics A and B stand facing each other in a room. A picks up a custard pie and outrageously lets B have it over the head. How do we show this simple action in a series of shots and how do we keep the sense of space continuous?

continuity of space

First of all, we are interested in A's extraordinary action, which will have its greatest impact if it comes in our direction. We frame A and B in the shot, but face the camera toward A (Fig. 13, position no. 1). If we film the entire action, we will have missed B's expression on the receiving end. So next we shoot the same action with a close-up of B's face (Fig. 13, position no. 2).

If we had two cameras, we could shoot both shots simultaneously with one pie, but with just one camera, B will have to get cleaned up and go through the whole routine again. First, we film the whole action in both shots; we do not pick up the second shot where we think it will begin on the

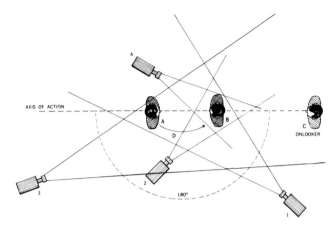

(*Fig.* 13) The axis of action and related camera angles. A—pie thrower; B—victim; C—onlooker; D—trajectory of pie; 1—master shot (MS); 2—reverse angle (CU); 3—reverse angle (LS); 4—reverse angle error (CU).

screen, but rather before. The action of the two shots must overlap so that the editor can choose the best moment to cut from A's pitch to B's expression. If this were a dialogue scene, we would also record the overlap in the dialogue on tape.

Other elements of continuity to keep in mind when matching two shots are maintaining actor, costume and prop position and detail, such as the length of a cigarette, or whether a jacket is open or closed.

From the first shot to the second, we changed both the camera position and the scope of the frame. Suppose we had not changed the camera position but had filmed a close-up of B by simply using a longer lens in the second shot. We would get only a side view of B's face, but—just as important—the effect would be a disconcerting jump to B when we followed the first shot to the second on the screen.

For a smooth and compelling flow of images, we need a change of shooting angle in the second shot as well as a change that will reveal more about the details of the action, which could be accomplished by going from a medium shot to a close-up. Another way to do this would be to take the second shot with a wider angle from farther back in the same direction (Fig. 13, position no. 3), showing a door opening behind B and the horrified expression of a third person (C) as A is about to throw the pie. This would change the shooting angle and the detail within the frame, and would also add a new element to the action.

When we took the close-up of B, what would have happened if we had taken it from the other side of the action, from camera position no. 4? In the first shot, position no. 1, B glances from right to left. In a shot taken from position no. 4, he would be looking from left to right. The effect of the two shots cut together would be discontinuous and would completely disorient the audience. In fact, it would seem as if B were a third person, not shown in the first shot, looking on from somewhere behind A, because B is now looking in the same direction as A in the first shot, from left to right.

Always keep your shots on the same side of the action. This has been called the 180-degree rule. Draw a line through the axis of the action (see Fig. 14): all your shots should be from the same side of the line, or from camera positions 1, 2 and 3. No matter how complicated the details of the action, this will give the viewer sufficient orientation to knit together the space of the film.

A special case of the foregoing is the reverse-angle shot. This shot entails a position change of a full half-circle from the shot preceding it, or the limit of the 180-degree rule. It is often used as a point-of-view shot which discloses what a character in the preceding shot is watching.

Let's suppose an exterior situation where our first shot is a close-up of someone looking in the direction of the camera. Our second shot can be a shot of any particular scene or object that the person might be observing. When we project the two shots on the screen, our experience will be that the second shot is what the subject saw when he looked in the direction of the camera in the first shot, even if the two shots have no object in common. One caution is not to have the character walk into the point-of-view shot since this will dispel the illusion that we, the audience, are seeing through his eyes.

SHOT =1   SHOT =4

(*Fig.* 14) Crossing the axis of action. If shot no. 1 is followed by shot no. 4, B will be confused with A or a third person.

continuity of time

Film time may be either compressed or expanded, depending upon the requirements of a particular situation. Let us note some examples.

Returning to the situation with the two comics, suppose we see the pie fall from B toward the floor in the second shot. In the third shot, we see a happy dog wander in and begin to lap up the pie. Shot number four is a close-up of A expressing disapproval and shot number five returns to the dog, who has finished the entire pie.

Film time essentially reflects real time in the first three shots. However, we need not concentrate on A in shot number four for a time that would realistically reflect the time it would take the dog to polish off the entire pie. It would just be boring in the finished film. A glance at A's expression is sufficient. Though this is a simple example, film time can tremendously compress real time in much the same way.

On the other hand, film time may expand real time, and this technique is usually used to increase suspense. Comic A raises the pie preparing to throw, but at this moment we cut away from A to a shot of B's look of amazement, then to the dog cowering in the corner, and so on. We can even expand the action further by a cut to a friend of B's coming up the stairs to the door behind A. B pleads with A not to throw the pie. A hesitates. B's friend, his fist raised, is about to knock on the door. . . . Audience suspense mounts as the details multiply, while in real time the pie would have long since been thrown.

continuity of motion

Suppose, after the dog has finished the pie, we see A walk out the door and disappear. Then in the next shot, we see him getting into a car. In both real time and space, there are missing chunks of information: how did he get to the car? And yet, in the film we would experience no sense of discontinuity. If our character leaves the frame, he can turn up in any likely place in the next shot, and our imagination leaps the gap. In this case, the continuity is supplied by following A.

An amusing short film can be made which nicely illustrates the last point. The film follows the adventures of a bouncing ball. If we let a ball bounce through a shot and out of the frame, and in each subsequent shot pick up the ball in some different location, allowing it to go out of the frame or disappear each time, the ball will take on a life of its own. Even though there is no continuity of real time or space (we see the ball magically appear in totally different locations), film continuity is maintained by following the bouncing ball.

continuity of an event: cutaways and reaction shots

Cutaways and reaction shots are shots which can be used to collapse the duration of an event.

Suppose you are filming an event such as a rock concert or a football game. Suppose further that there are parts of the event which are uninteresting or that you did not even film. How do you cut together the portions that you want to use and still make the event look continuous?

The solution is to take shots of related activity and fill the gaps with these. Shots taken for this purpose are called cutaways. The most common example is the shot of the onlooker. If he is reacting to what is happening in the event—applauding, for example—we call it a reaction shot. When shooting an event, always cover yourself by shooting cutaway material so that the editor can afford to be selective in his use of the main action.

parallel action

Parallel action is where a number of different but related events take place simultaneously. For example, in the old Western, the heroine is being tied to the tracks by the villain while the train approaches around the bend, and the hero rides to the rescue. Even though we film the heroine, the approaching train and the hero as entirely separate events, when we cut them together, alternating between the victim's plight, the oncoming train and the rescue chase, they will be experienced as simultaneous events. Cutting back and forth between events is also a way of collapsing the events themselves. If we see the villain make the first knot, then cut to the approaching train, and then to the hero, the heroine can be completely bound when we cut back again.

In chapter 2, we discussed the use of the storyboard. No other planning approach makes the filmmaker so aware of the flow of images. He must account for how he gets from one shot to the next, and in doing so, he must concern himself with the problems of film continuity.

camera movement

So far we have discussed shots only in terms of the framing, as in long shots, medium shots and close-ups. We need not necessarily cut from shot to shot, from detail to detail; we can move the camera. If we move the camera *while shooting*, there is no axis of action that we cannot cross; there is no discontinuity of time or space because the moving shot provides us with a continual reference. Our chief concern then becomes what action or detail we want to reveal in the shot.

the pan

The most common camera movement is called a pan, derived from the word panorama. This is a horizontal rotation of the camera on its axis whereby the camera remains in a fixed position—usually mounted on a tripod—but is directed from one side to another. In general, the motivation for this type of movement is when a subject moves to the right or left of the beginning frame. A good panning movement leads the subject, so that most of the frame area remains to the front of the subject. If the movement is smooth, we will not notice the pan but will be involved in the movement of the subject and the unfolding of new detail in the scene. It should flow with the action. If the movement is jerky, we will become aware of mechanics and be distracted from the action.

There are other important uses of the pan. Instead of staying with the subject, we may want to shift the emphasis of the scene; for example, panning from the subject to the entry of a new character, or revealing a detail which changes the course or impact of a scene. Panning from a detective to his partially hidden suspect combines both examples.

When used in this fashion, the pan illustrates a keen sense of space and precisely points up the new element. Or a pan may be truly panoramic and used to show more of a scene than any static establishing shot could do. In panning from a foreground object to a distant horizon, the movement can give the impact of tremendous depth to a scene.

A pan over static objects has one important limitation: the movement must be slow. A fast pan causes a visual distortion of the screen image, known as "skipping." The pan literally seems to skip from one area of space to the next instead of moving continuously. This distortion is emphasized if the subject matter is composed of vertical lines, such as a white picket fence. The chances of skipping are reduced under these conditions: the slower the pan, the farther the camera from the subject and the wider the angle of the lens.

The use of long lenses for panning is restricted to the case where we are following, and the frame is mostly filled with a moving object. Our interest is held by the moving object rather than the static background, and skipping will not occur, particularly if the background is in soft focus. This type of shot can be very useful when we are otherwise unable to move with our subject. For instance, if we want to follow our subject as he moves past several

(*Photo* 64) Camera leading the action. When subject moves laterally in front of the camera, camera keeps more space in front of subject than behind. It anticipates the direction in which the action will move and leaves room for it.

shop windows on a crowded street, we can set up the camera with a telephoto lens across the street, and appear to be moving alongside of him.

If a pan is extremely fast, objects between the beginning and the final point of the pan will be blurred. This is called a swish pan, and can be used for a highly dramatic effect when it reveals something with an element of surprise. However, it is difficult to pan quickly and arrive rock-steady at a final frame. Most swish pans are artificial, and accomplished by ending one shot with a lightning pan and then *cutting* to a new shot before the swish pan is completed.

the tilt

As with the pan, the camera remains in a fixed position when tilting, but the direction is changed vertically. We tilt up from the subject to a skyscraper, or down from the subject's face to the paper at his feet. Skipping presents a similar problem for this movement, and the solutions are the same: slow movement, use of the wider focal-length lenses, increase the camera-to-subject distance.

Like the pan, it should lead subject movement in the vertical plane: sitting down, getting up, climbing stairs. It can be used to reveal detail—tilting down from a look of disgust to the food on the plate —though its most dramatic use is in the revelation of height—tilting up the side of a skyscraper or down from the side of a cliff. The angle of a static shot is often hard to judge, but if we tilt from an object whose angle or perspective is known (a standing figure at the base of a cliff), the sensation of height is made more real.

zooming

When zoom lenses were discussed in chapter 4, the movement of constantly increasing or decreasing focal length was described as zooming in or zooming out. The resulting change of frame size is comparable to moving closer to or farther away from the subject. But the camera itself does not move, and when we see the shot on the screen, we miss the excitement of the moving shot. The effect is optical only since we do not really move in relation to the object.

Because of the optical effect of the zoom movement, the editor may simply use the beginning and end of the zoom shot for a change in frame size, or cut from a medium shot to a close-up, while leaving out the zoom movement. However, if the zoom is used in conjunction with a camera pan or tilt and, in particular, if the shot is not simply panoramic but follows action, the optical effect is less obvious and the appearance of real movement is greatly increased.

The most objectionable use of the zoom is in a static situation where the cameraman zooms into significant detail. You feel like you have been hit over the head. News cameramen at art exhibitions are constantly zooming into details of paintings they think you should look at. In the end we are only distracted by this abrupt motion and never actually see the paintings.

the dolly shot

A dolly is a platform on wheels that moves the camera and, with it, the camera operator. Most dollies can be moved in a straight line in any direction or steered in a circular movement. Documentary cameramen, who must constantly be inventive, have used everything from wheelchairs to shopping carts to propel the camera smoothly. A rough dolly shot is like a jerky pan—distracting. Soft tires will help to some extent, but for a steady movement, the surface over which the dolly passes really must be smooth. When you are not shooting in a studio, you can cover the floor with large sheets of plywood or masonite.

The movement of a dolly shot is exciting because it involves us in feeling the space within the frame. When the camera is actually moving, all points in the space of the frame are constantly changing in relation to one another. What this means is that all the objects in the scene seem to be constantly changing in shape, and our eyes are being fed a constant stream of information about their size and texture. No matter how masterfully a zoom is executed, it can never give us this three-dimensional sense.

tracking and crane shots

A tracking shot is made by using a dolly which is constructed to run on tracks. Tracks, not as heavy as but similar to railroad tracks, must be laid for the entire length of the shot. This kind of shot is often used in feature films, for example, where two characters must be followed close at hand as they walk in conversation for some distance along the beach or a path or any other rough terrain where a dolly would be unsuitable. If you are lucky enough to have a road nearby, and if the characters are walking along a sidewalk, you can use a car with soft springs to transport the cameraman who can shoot from an open door or window.

A crane shot involves a motorized crane with a position at the head for the cameraman. The movement is special since it is not related to our normal experience, and the effect can be quite dramatic, such as when the camera sweeps up in a great arc to reveal the entire scene of a crime, or when, in Hitchcock's *Psycho*, it swooped down on the victim like a giant bird. Some dollies have an elevator mechanism which will raise the camera a few feet. To the same effect, a hand-held camera can be raised from a kneeling to a standing position. Both these movements have their own kinetic excitement, and the latter, in particular, is recommended.

vehicle speed vs. screen speed

When shooting from a moving vehicle such as a car, and the camera is at right angles to the direction the car takes, the speed of the screen image will appear greater the longer the focal length of the lens. The opposite is true when filming in the same direction as the vehicle: the wider the angle of the lens, the greater the apparent speed will seem.

The effect you want will determine the focal length of the lens you use. For example, if you are shooting a profile of the driver and you want the background to flash by, use as long a focal length as you can. If you are shooting in the same direction as the car and want the effect of speed, use a wide-angle lens.

following focus and completing the movement

Moving shots often involve a change in subject-to-camera distance. In particular, when panning from a near to a distant object or with a subject moving toward or away from the camera, the shift in focus may be considerable. The depth of field of your shot, or what is actually in focus, may accommodate the difference. If it does not, you will have to "follow focus." This means that you will change the point of critical focus during the shot by actually focusing the lens while the camera is running.

Documentary cameramen must often do this reflexively while shooting, and learn to adjust the focusing ring on the lens while observing the shift in focus in the reflex viewing system. This takes some amount of skill to do correctly. If you are shooting something which is staged, the extremes of focus can be found before shooting and marked on the focusing ring with a grease pencil. During the shot, an assistant can then make the change of focus.

When planning a moving shot, you should be aware of its duration and the effect of its pacing on a given scene. Since it is difficult to preserve a sense of continuity and cut from a moving shot to a static one (exceptions to this will be discussed in the chapter on editing), you should learn to complete the movement of the shot gracefully, without dwelling too long. Particularly in documentary shooting, where you must often pan with the movement of an unpredictable subject, learn when to let him walk out of frame so that the editor will have enough leeway to choose an appropriate cutting point.

tripod vs. hand-held shooting

When a camera is hand-held, there will always be a certain amount of body movement communicated in the shot. This is distracting, because it makes you aware of how the film was made and not what the film is saying. Because their weight makes them easy to support, 8mm cameras are usually hand-held. But then, it is not necessary for 8mm films to meet the stringent requirements of professional work. When working in 16mm, however, the camera weight becomes a critical factor, and shooting from a tripod should be the rule unless the hand-held position is necessitated by the nature of the shot or the desired effect of the film.

Tripods are three-legged camera supports. The important part of the tripod is the head, since this is the part that will determine the quality of a panning or tilting movement. The best heads have a hydraulic, or geared, operation, which insures a continuously smooth pan or tilt. These are called fluid, or gyro, heads, which are fairly expensive—costing several hundred dollars. Less expensive tripods are equipped with friction heads, which are difficult to use without introducing a jerky movement.

Hand-held work in 16mm is justified under certain conditions. If the style of the film is cinéma vérité—that is, with no rehearsed action—the movement of the subject of the film is not restricted, and the cameraman must follow whenever and wherever the subject chooses. The camera is usually mounted on the cameraman's shoulder by means of a brace. This distributes the weight of the camera over the whole body rather than on the arms alone.

Whenever the documentary cameraman is faced with quickly changing and unpredictable action, he has to be free to follow immediately. If he is working from a tripod, he cannot continue to shoot, but must pick up the tripod and move it. Not only that, but every time he sets the tripod down, he must adjust the level of the head so that the horizontal line of the frame coincides with the horizontal line of the scene or the horizon. On some tripods, this means laboriously adjusting the length of the legs. Better tripods have a quick-leveling bowl mechanism at the base of the head. In any case, he stands a good chance of losing the action. If the camera is hand-held, he has only to move himself.

The appearance of body movement in the screened image is minimized when the camera is used to follow action. It is maximized when the camera must be held steady on a static subject for any length of time. In this situation, it is best to wedge your body against a wall or any other solid object. Sometimes body movement is used intentionally to communicate the turbulence of an action sequence. Sometimes only the quick movements permitted by hand-held photography are sufficient to catch close-up details.

However, aside from these specific situations where action is the key, a pan or a tilt can be a beautiful and graceful movement only when made from the right kind of tripod.

composition and framing

In a still photograph, our eye is primarily drawn by the beauty and balance of the graphic composition. In a motion picture, our eye is primarily drawn by the movement within the frame. When a shot not only frames the action well, but also composes a beautiful graphic balance, the best possible result of the cameraman's art has been achieved.

The image on the screen is two-dimensional, and yet the movement within it creates a feeling of depth. Film composition must emphasize this depth, for this is what draws our attention into the frame and makes watching motion pictures an exciting experience. Besides movement of the camera itself, there are three major considerations to emphasize depth when composing a frame: direction of subject action, blocking of foreground and background objects and lighting differentiations.

Movement toward and away from the camera involves the viewer more than lateral action in the depth of the frame: the subject disappears down a road and moves away from the camera; the rush of an attack comes toward the camera. Movement toward and away from the camera will be emphasized by lenses with wider focal lengths. A long lens will compact the action.

If the subject moves laterally, or across the frame, a wide-angle lens will make his progress look slower, while a long lens can make the background flash by. (This is the same situation as described earlier when making a shot from a car at right angles to its direction.)

(*Photo* 65) Composition with foreground detail helps create a sense of depth.

Composition that sets off foreground and background objects gives a great feeling of depth to a scene. Scenes shot through foreground grass or leaves are one example, though more important, in a dramatic sense, is the blocking of the principals between foreground and background in a scene. The tension between them seems to be heightened by the feeling of depth.

Lastly, the sense of depth in a scene can be heightened by creating zones of lighting which are differentiated as the eye is drawn back into the frame. The simplest use of this effect is where the background is darker or lighter than the subject in the foreground. Similarly, back and side lighting increase the sense of separation and, therefore, the depth. A completely dark room will seem flat, but a corridor filled with shadowy areas of dark and light can appear endless.

The angle of a shot is also an important concern of composition, since this will affect the way the subject will appear. An eye-level shot has the perspective of normal vision. When we go above that level, the shot is called a high-angle shot, and the effect makes the subject look less dominant and more vulnerable. A shot made from a considerable height makes a person's progress appear antlike, and he seems to be more under the control of circumstances than his own will. On the other hand, a low-angle shot—one made from ground level, for instance—makes the subject look dominant and powerful, as if nothing could stop him. Orson Welles used low-angle photography effectively in *Citizen Kane.*

The job of framing the action or subject depends so much on the specific case that it is difficult to set up any general rules. However, a few observations can be made. If we can see the person's face, we don't mind his being cut off at the shoulders, chest or waist, but it begins to look strange if we cut him

Satyajit Ray's *Two Daughters*, courtesy of Janus Films

(*Photo* 66) The creation of depth within a frame by blocking or placing the actors between foreground and background

off at the knees, and definitely discomforting if we cut off only his feet. If we see his torso or full figure, there should be sufficient head room so the shot won't have a cramped feeling.

In framing action, the composition should unfold in the direction of the action. If someone is throwing something toward the right of the frame, he should then be in the left of the frame, leaving the right open. This kind of framing leads the action in the direction of our anticipations.

Everything need not be shown. A hand with a gun is enough to show what frightens the man in the background. If two people are talking and we want to concentrate on the face of one of them, the back of the shoulder and side of the head is sufficient to establish the presence of the other.

setting up

When using Super 8mm, merely snap the cartridge into place and the camera is ready to use. With a 16mm camera using a 100-foot daylight spool, the first step after threading the film is to run in the first five feet to get past any film that might have been exposed in the loading operation. This will usually get a few feet past the exposed portion, so do not waste this film. Use this footage to film a sheet of paper with your name on it and the title of the film. If things should get mixed up in the lab, this will identify your film. In a professional production, this information would be written on a slate with a piece of chalk. What you are doing then is called "slating."

After you have run in and slated, you should check the camera aperture, which you can do after removing the lens. This should be done at this time because lint or dust on the head of the film or

Ian Dunlop's documentary *Desert People*, courtesy of Contemporary Films/McGraw-Hill

(*Photo* 67) Dramatic composition draws the eye into the frame.

inside the camera tends to catch in the aperture with the first five feet of film. All this might sound unnecessary until you have had a few of your best shots ruined by a piece of lint caught at the frame line. After you have replaced the lens, you will be ready to frame your first shot.

shooting with sound

In 16mm, there are two methods of shooting with sound: single system and double system. Single-system sound is used by newsmen since it is not designed for the creative use of sound, but to record, as simply as possible, the sound that occurs with the picture. The raw stock used has a magnetic stripe on the edge and, inside the camera, a recording head records the sound on this stripe as the picture is being taken. As mentioned before, television stations use the camera original for convenience, and single-system sound provides the economy of sound directly accompanying the picture.

Single-system sound has now been made available in Super 8 with the introduction of a new Kodak camera which utilizes either 50- or 200-foot film cartridges that are prestriped with a magnetic track. Incorporated in the camera is a sound-recording system with an automatic volume, or modulation, control. By using an omnidirectional microphone which comes with the camera, sound is recorded on the magnetic track simultaneously with the Super 8 picture. The whole unit weighs less than four pounds and costs about $425.

It should be noted that, in single-system sound, the input from the microphone is recorded on the film in advance of the picture. Since the sound-

Ingmar Bergman's *The Virgin Spring*, courtesy of Janus Films

(*Photo* 68) The creation of depth within a frame by differentiated zones of lighting

Ingmar Bergman's *The Seventh Seal*, courtesy of Janus Films

(*Photo* 69) Darkened background sets off dramatic composition in foreground. Note also the modeling produced by side lighting on foreground subjects.

recording head cannot be placed at the camera gate, the sound is recorded 18 frames in front of the picture in Super 8, and 28 frames in 16mm. This has a certain drawback: in editing the film, approximately a full second of sound at the head of a shot will be cut off. Similarly, the tail of the shot will contain the same amount of sound (18 frames) from the subsequent shot. This momentary mismatch of picture and sound—when making a cut—cannot match the precision of double-system sound, but it is acceptable for news, student or home movies.

For filming other than newsreel work, double-system sound is used. With this system, sound is recorded separately on a tape recorder, which not only permits higher quality, but the facility of dealing with the sound separately in the editing process (see chapter 11). The question is how do we obtain synchronous sound—sound that can be played back exactly in time with the picture—when the tape recorder runs independently of the camera? (Synchronous or sync sound is sound that can be played back exactly in time with the picture.)

There are a number of techniques that have been developed to solve this problem. The most common is the use of a sync pulse which is transmitted from the camera to the tape recorder. In this case, the camera will be equipped with a battery-powered constant-speed motor which generates a periodic sync pulse. The pulse is carried to the tape recorder by means of a cable or a tiny radio transmitter. At the tape recorder, the pulse, which you do not hear, is recorded on the tape whenever the camera is in operation, and provides a record of the camera motor's speed. Chapter 11 will deal with the transfer of the $\frac{1}{4}$-inch recording tape to 16mm magnetic stock which can then be linked with the picture.

A second method is to use a synchronous motor

Orson Welles's *Citizen Kane,* courtesy of Janus Films

(*Photo* 70) *Citizen Kane* was remarkable for many innovations, not the least of which was its use of low-angle photography.

on the camera which is powered not by batteries but by AC current, and its speed is governed by the 60-cycle pulse of the AC current. With a separate transformer, the tape recorder records the same 60-cycle pulse. When the tape is then transferred to 16mm magnetic stock, the recorded 60-cycle pulse is used to match the speed of the transfer to the camera speed.

The third technique is the latest development and is quickly gaining popularity. It utilizes crystal-controlled motors in both the camera and the tape recorder, insuring, in both cases, the constancy of the motor's speed and eliminating the need for a cable or radio transmission between the camera and the tape recorder, as well as any dependency on AC power. What is needed, then, is only a start signal at the beginning of each shot which will be common to both camera and tape recorder.

start mark

In addition to identifying the beginning of each camera roll, the slate is also used to identify the beginning of each sound take. At the top of the slate is a clapstick. With the camera and the recorder both running, the clapstick is banged sharply against the top of the slate. The sound of the clap is recorded by the tape recorder and simultaneously filmed by the camera at the instant the clapstick and top of the slate come together. This provides a start signal so that the picture can later be linked up with the sound in the editing room.

In documentary work, the use of the clapstick may be an unwanted intrusion into the filming situation. A mechanical technique has therefore

(*Photos* 71, 72) Low angle (left) makes figure appear dominant. High angle (right) makes figure seem passive.

been developed whereby the first few frames of each shot are exposed by a light inside the camera. This exposure is transmitted to the tape recorder by means of the sync cable or transmitter, where it is recorded as a "beep" of the same duration.

Remember, once the start mark has been recorded by whatever means, the camera or tape recorder cannot be stopped and started again without the recording of an additional start mark. This can also be done at the very end of a take, in which case the slate is called a tail slate.

super 8 sync sound

Until recently, double-system sound had been unavailable in Super 8. However, a number of systems have now appeared on the market. Two of them are quite similar in operation to 16mm sync-sound systems. The MIT/Leacock system, developed by Richard Leacock at MIT and manufactured by Hampton Engineering of Norwood, Massachusetts, has modified a Nizo Super 8 camera to incorporate a crystal-controlled running speed of 24 fps. A companion Sony cassette recorder is also crystal controlled. The Nizo camera is blimped so that it can be used without transmitting camera noise to the recorder.

Beaulieu also makes a Super 8 camera which will generate a sync pulse and can be used in conjunction with a Uher tape recorder.

Another of the new systems, the Super 8 Sound System, introduced a note of change in its method of recording sound. Its Sony tape recorder uses magnetic tape which is identical in gauge and sprocket-hole pattern to Super 8 film. In this system, the speed of the recorder is "slaved" to the

camera speed by means of a sync-pulse cable.

Yet another system, marketed by Optasound Corporation of New York City, utilizes a cassette recorder and perforated magnetic tape. The perforations in the tape are read by a lamp in the recorder and a signal is sent by cable to the camera so that one frame is exposed for each perforation on the tape.

Although sync sound systems are still relatively expensive, Super 8 still has the advantage for the beginner of very great savings over 16mm on the cost of raw stock and processing.

Besides involving us, sound gives the picture continuity. It takes the separate shots that make up a sequence and threads them together, giving them a single, unbroken, rather than separate, reality. The simplest sound—for example, wind or footsteps—gives us a key, or cue, a reference to continuity. Without this reference, shots remain separate bits of geography, and we are left without a guide through time.

Just as important as this reference to continuity is sound's capacity to indicate discontinuity. If one shot is accompanied by the sound of traffic and the next by wind alone, we know we have been transported to a totally different space. This information does not have to be given at all by the visual image. A simple change in the sound key tells us all we need to know.

Early films used the advent of sound on film to record dialogue. Sound was seen simply as a means of supplying the words in the script. They were aptly called "talkies." Indeed, the simplest use of sound is to record the reality of the image. That is, if we see something that would seem to make sound in the picture, that sound should be heard on the sound track. Actually, the use of sound can be far more complex and far more interesting.

Robert Flaherty's *Nanook of the North*, courtesy of Contemporary Films/McGraw-Hill

(*Photo* 73) The composition is balanced to anticipate the thrust of the hunter's arm.

We have already seen how certain key sounds are used to tell us where we are. Every sound editor knows that if a film calls for cutting back and forth between two or more locations, each location should have a distinct sound reference so that the audience knows immediately where it is. Key sounds can also set up the atmosphere of a sequence. They can make it mysterious—the cry of a strange bird, peaceful—the rhythmic sound of rippling water, or upsetting—the din of city traffic or loud machinery.

Off-screen sounds are sometimes more important than the sounds of what is happening on the screen. A familiar example is the scream of the victim who has not yet been seen, or the whistle of the train that has not yet arrived. The peaceful scene of a mother nursing her baby can be quickly changed by the sound of a siren from outside. The ringing of a telephone or doorbell, the creaking of a floorboard or the barking of a dog can all trigger important changes in a scene.

These examples indicate the use of sound for dramatic emphasis. Take the common situation in a mystery movie where an unknown assailant has been following one of the principal characters home. As the pace of the footsteps increases, so does our suspense. At the right moment, a pause of silence will greatly heighten our experience of anxiety. If a pause is followed by the crash of breaking glass as the assailant invades the sanctuary of the home, we will invariably react with a leap in our hearts, if not out of our seats.

Sound can also be used thematically. In Fritz Lang's early classic sound movie, *M*, the murderer is known for some time only by the strange tune he whistles. The tune at once creates the atmosphere of the film and identifies the main character. The most common use of thematic sound is, of course, theme music, music used to set the mood of the film.

(*Photo* 74) Slate, or clapstick. The sound made by the hinged top as it is dropped is recorded by the tape recorder and will be lined up with the corresponding frame of the picture where the slate closes to establish sync. The numbers identify the scene and take.

Sound can also become a symbol. For example, the frustration of a character's inability to escape a situation could be accompanied by the increasing noise of machinery; or the echo of footsteps in a deserted street might emphasize a character's loneliness and despair. In *Sundays and Cybelle*, the two main characters skip stones across an ice pond. The sound of the stones on the ice seemed to tell us exactly how isolated their worlds were.

summary

When you shoot your film, you must have in mind the flow of images. If you know how each shot connects with the ones preceding and following it, then you will know how to frame and pace your shooting. Use a storyboard to work out the continuity of film space and time. Don't content yourself with one long shot that records all the action like a stage play. Film alternate angles, close-up details of the action, cutaways and reaction shots, so that you can work out a compelling sequence of shots in the editing room.

Panning and tilting are the most common camera movements, and are best made from a tripod equipped with a fluid, or gyro, head. A dolly actually puts the camera in motion, giving the shot a visual excitement for which zooming is a poor substitute. Tracking and crane shots have their place in the flow of images, but require elaborate equipment that is not practical or advisable for the beginner.

Hand-held camera work communicates distracting body movement to the shot, but is justified where the documentary cameraman cannot predict the movement of the subject or the action.

Composition must not only frame action, but must emphasize the feeling of depth. It is the visual depth of a frame that gives movement in motion pictures a three-dimensional excitement. Depth is obtained by directing the action into the frame, blocking foreground and background objects, and differentiating background space by lighting. If a pleasing graphic balance is also achieved in the shot, you will have accomplished the best of the cameraman's art.

Checking the camera, loading the film, running in and slating the roll are the first steps in setting up to shoot. If you are shooting with sound, you will have to slate the beginning of each shot for identification, and provide a start mark for matching the picture to sound in the editing process.

Single-system sound records the sound on the side of the film and is used for news reporting. Double-system sound records the sound separately on a tape recorder. The speed of the tape recorder and camera are either linked by a sync pulse or governed by a crystal control.

8. SOUND: ANOTHER DIMENSION

the uses of sound with film: involvement and continuity, dramatic, thematic, metaphorical emphasis • sound techniques: synchronous and wild sound • modulation • compression • the microphone • recording speech • recording sound effects • the soundman's job

The single most underrated aspect of film is the sound track. Turn down the volume on a television set, and most of what you see will look absurd and unrelated, even if it is a highly exciting action sequence. You will quickly become bored. The early silent films were never really "silent"; besides the written dialogue captions, they were generally accompanied by a piano player. This helped create the normal coupling of sight and sound that we expect in life. Sound takes the observer from outside—peering in through the window—and leads him into the room. It helps us feel that we are actually present in the reality on the screen.

There are two kinds of sound whose source we never see on the screen, but nevertheless completely accept: narration, which may guide us through an entire film, and the musical score, much of which we might not even consciously notice.

Theme music is an offshoot and elaboration of the role of the piano player who accompanied silent movies. It is often used excessively and in an overbearing manner. By telling us exactly how we should feel at a given moment, it frequently spoils a subtler dramatic effect. Nevertheless, it is an accepted convention of much film production, and its popularity is based on the fact that, when used well, theme music alone can accomplish most of the above-noted functions of sound with film.

Sometimes music is the very substance of a film, such as in a musical, the biography of a famous composer, *Woodstock*, or the Beatles' films, *Hard Day's Night* and *Help*.

There is also a special use of music which has particular relevance to the short film, the form with which you will most likely be involved, at least in the beginning. This is called cutting to music. The entire sound track of a short film can consist of a single piece of music. If the shots are timed to the music, and especially if the shots are short and the rhythm is lively, the effect can be amusing and entertaining. The action on the screen seems to be animated by the music in a comical fashion. Shots can be made to pop on and off as if impelled by the rhythm (see chapter 11).

sound technique

In terms of film production, there are two kinds of sound: synchronous (or sync) sound and wild sound. Sync sound means that sound was recorded in such a way while filming that it can be played back exactly in time with the image on the screen. Wild sound is sound recorded independently of filming, often at a different time and place.

In this chapter, we will concern ourselves with the process of recording, which is the same for sync as for wild sound.

Most sound now used in motion pictures is originally recorded on a portable tape recorder like the Nagra (photo 1). Exceptions would be where a sound effect or music is taken from a phonograph record, or where voices, music or sound effects are recorded with the facilities of a sound studio. Whatever the various designs of the portable tape recorder, its function is basically the same.

A reel of ¼-inch recording tape, usually five inches in diameter holding 600 feet of tape, is placed on spindle A of the recorder (Fig. 15), and taken up on spindle B on a similar 5-inch reel. The tape itself is much lighter and narrower than film and has no sprocket holes. It is composed of an iron oxide coating, or dull side, on an acetate or polyester base, the shiny side. (On the newest 3M-brand low-noise tape, which is black rather than the usual brown, the shiny side is the emulsion and the dull side is the base.) When you are ready to record, a switch starts the motor and engages the tape with anywhere from two to four *heads* (Fig. 15, 1 to 4).

Going from A to B, the tape first passes head No.

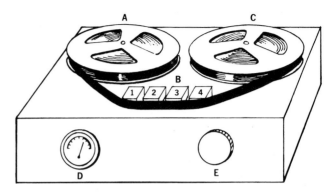

(*Fig.* 15) The tape recorder. A—tape feed; B—heads: 1—erase, 2—record, 3—sync, 4—playback; C—tape take-up; D—record-level meter; E—volume control

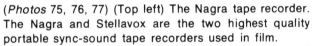

(*Photos* 75, 76, 77) (Top left) The Nagra tape recorder. The Nagra and Stellavox are the two highest quality portable sync-sound tape recorders used in film.

(Bottom left) The Stellavox with headset and external power transformer. Each model costs about $2,000. (Top right) The Sony 800B. This is an excellent tape recorder in the under-$300 range.

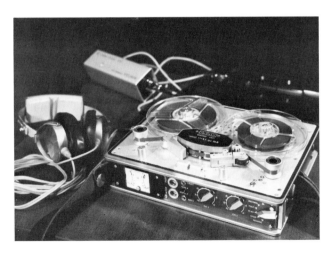

1. This is generally an erase head which will eliminate any prior recording. It prevents the mistake of a garbled double recording and enables you to use a tape more than once.

Head No. 2 is the record head. The sound received by the microphone is turned into an electrical signal. The record head sends the signal to the tape, transforming it into a magnetic pattern which can later be reproduced.

If the tape recorder is equipped to record sync sound, then head No. 3 will be the sync head. When the tape passes this head, a sync signal is recorded. It cannot be heard, but is generated by the camera to provide a record of the camera's speed. This is explained in greater detail in chapters 7 and 11.

On an inexpensive recorder, head No. 2 will double as the record head and the playback head. If the recorder has a separate playback head (Fig. 15, head No. 4), then you will be able to monitor, or test, and adjust the recording while it is being made. The playback is almost instantaneous, the signal passing the playback head a fraction of a second after it has been recorded, and by using a set of earphones, you can hear any distortion in the recording which may have been introduced by heads No. 2 and 3.

Depending upon the tape recorder, the motor may run at one constant speed or at a variety of speeds: $3^1/_4$ inches/second is suitable for amateur work, while most professional recording is done at $7^1/_2$ inches/second. The more tape that is used per word, or the faster the speed of the tape, the easier it is to make a cut, since the space between words will be greater. Also, the faster the speed of the tape, the higher the quality of the recorded sound will be.

modulation

On the front of the tape recorder there will be a volume control for modulating, i.e., decreasing or increasing, the strength of the signal coming from the microphone. Most poor sound recording is due to overmodulation, or having the volume control set too high for the capacity of the recording system. This will cause distortion. Every tape recorder has some way to measure the incoming signal so that this can be avoided.

Professional tape recorders and some amateur equipment will come equipped with a record-level meter, which measures the incoming signal in decibels (dbs) on a dial with a needle indicator. A db is the smallest change in strength of a sound that the human ear can discriminate. A change of 6 dbs means that the signal has either doubled or halved in strength.

The dial of the meter will indicate the level of maximum tolerance for the system. In figure 15 this occurs at 0 db. Normally, you record at a level of -6 dbs, or with a signal of half the maximum strength. When a person speaks, he modulates his voice for emphasis and intonation. If his average level is set at -6 dbs, then most of the peaks of his speech will be within the maximum tolerance of the recorder. An occasional peak past the maximum level is to be expected.

Many amateur recorders will not be equipped with a record-level meter, but with a signal light instead. A common system is where one-half of a flashing light indicates a signal of sufficient strength for recording. When the signal overmodulates, both halves will light up for as long as the signal is above maximum strength, or until the volume control is turned down.

When recording, there are several simple rules to follow when setting the volume control. Professional tape recorders usually have a test position, a position that can be used before the motor starts, to measure the incoming signal from the microphone. Always measure the strength of the signal you are going to record *before* you record it. This will enable you to set the volume control at a safe level and leave it there during the recording.

Never move the volume control during the recording, since you will find the changes it will cause to be very noticeable and distracting when you play back the recording. If you must make a change, do it very gradually.

Some tape recorders have an automatic position which ensures safety from overmodulation. When locked in this position, a very loud signal will be instantaneously and automatically lowered to an acceptable level. However, because this device causes numerous changes in the level of background noise and a loss in sound fidelity, it is not generally used for recordings of professional quality.

compression

Just as the eye can tolerate greater differences in brightness than film, the human ear can tolerate sounds of varying intensities much better than your tape recorder. For example, if you are recording a piece of music which has passages that build from quiet to medium and loud, you will find that there is no one recording level that will do a satisfactory job on the whole piece. So you should set the level for the medium passage and learn to anticipate the changes to quiet or loud music with gradual changes of the volume control. In recording terminology, this process is known as compression because you actually compress the intensity of the louder passages.

the microphone

Other causes of poorly recorded sound quality have to do with the placement and handling of the microphone. Microphones have different characteristics and fall basically into four categories: omnidirectional; cardioid, or unidirectional; shotgun, or ultradirectional; and the lavalier.

The sensitivity pattern of the omnidirectional microphone (Fig. 16, A) gives equal emphasis to sound coming from anywhere around the microphone. This characteristic is useful for recording a round-table discussion group, an orchestra or a general presence, as in the sound of a crowd or the ambience of a marketplace.

A cardioid (heart-shaped) microphone is the most useful single microphone to have. Its sensitivity pattern (Fig. 16, B) de-emphasizes sound to the side and the rear of the direction in which the microphone is pointed. It is the best microphone to record two or three people in conversation, the music of a small band and most sound effects.

The shotgun microphone is noted for its narrow band of sensitivity (Fig. 16, C). Shotgun microphones are popular in documentary work because of their capacity to be fairly discriminatory when pointed in the direction of the sound source; for example, they can be used to pick one person out of a crowd or discussion group.

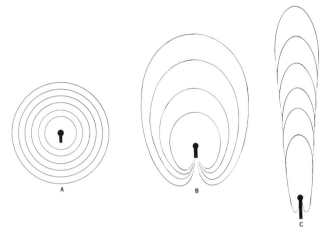

(*Fig.* 16) Basic microphone receptivity patterns: A—omnidirectional; B—cardioid; C—shotgun

Somewhat comparable to the omnidirectional microphone in sensitivity, the lavalier microphone is designed to hang around the speaker's neck in the middle of the chest. It is useful because the speaker can move with the microphone attached and never change the critical distance between his voice and the microphone. The chief drawback of the lavalier is that it tends to record the rustle of clothing.

If the microphone is held by hand or on a boom, a pole extension, the microphone must move when the speaker moves. This sometimes results in having to devise elaborate maneuvers to avoid showing the microphone or its shadow in the shot.

recording speech

In addition to adjusting modulation, microphone placement is the other critical concern in recording. If the microphone is too far away from the person speaking, his voice will be lost in the noise of the background. If it is too close, there will be a distortion of the voice's frequency range and an emphasis of sibilance, the hissing sound of an exaggerated S.

As a general guide to recording speech, keep the microphone an arm's length in front of the person speaking, slightly above or below the level of his head and pointed toward his mouth or chest. You can figure out the best precise placement by testing. When a person's sibilance is pronounced, a slight movement of the microphone to one side or the other of the head will lessen the harsh hissing quality of the voice. The lavalier is usually placed about halfway down the chest, and is either hung by a cord or pinned to the clothes.

When recording speech, there are two environmental conditions for which you should take caution. The first is background noise. Sufficient background noise will be distracting and will "muddy" the speech so that it is hard to understand. The remedy is to move to a quieter location; but if you have no choice, move the microphone as close to the speaker as possible without getting it into the shot or emphasizing the speaker's sibilance by positioning the microphone too close to his mouth.

In this respect, lavaliers are useful, especially those of recent design, which are no larger than the filter on a cigarette and are easy to hide on the speaker's clothing. Television personalities often wear them unobtrusively on tie clips or lapels. These microphones maintain a constantly close position to the speaker and consequently de-emphasize background noise.

The second condition to guard against is known as "boominess." This is a muddy quality of the lower and middle vocal range that is caused by reverberation. If the speaker is close to solid, hard surfaces, the lower and middle frequencies of his voice will be reflected back into the microphone's sensitivity pattern. The higher the frequency, the less the sound will be reflected. Lower frequencies in particular tend to "roll around" inside a room and muddy their distinctness.

If you are outdoors, do not record the speaker against the wall of a building. A shotgun microphone, in particular, will emphasize boominess in this situation. If you are indoors, do no record the speaker in the corner of a room, since this is where the reverberation is most concentrated. When recording sound, a room with carpets and drapery is preferable to one without. The more porous the material there is, the less the sounds will reverberate. The acoustics in a recording situation are very important to the quality of the sound.

recording sound effects

When recording sound effects, there are a few situations which may cause you trouble. Sounds which have the characteristic of a click or bang have a very high energy level; that is, they are very loud for a very short period of time. For this reason the tape recorder's meter or signal may not measure them accurately, so it is wise to monitor your recording and play it back. If the sound seems at all distorted, lower the volume control and record again.

Other sounds, like the rustle of clothing, have a low energy level and are very quiet. If you turn the volume control all the way up to get a stronger signal, you will begin to hear the noise or hiss inherent in the tape recorder. The better the set, the less interference you will hear. Your aim should be to keep this hiss acceptably quiet and still obtain a signal that is sufficiently strong for recording. This relationship is referred to as the signal-to-noise ratio.

Some sounds may be too loud for the microphone input circuit to handle. No adjustment of the volume control—no matter how low—will help, since the signal is distorted at its very inception. The signal goes through the microphone input circuit before it reaches the volume control on its way to the record head. If you dampen, or reduce, a signal at the stage of the volume control which is already distorted, you will end up with a sound that is less loud but still distorted. For example, this can happen when a person is shouting close to a microphone. If you have a correct modulation indication, but the sound still seems distorted, move the microphone back from the source until a clear sound is obtained.

Avoid handling the microphone during recording, if possible. If the microphone is hand-held, then do not change your grip. The vibrations from handling the microphone body or cable will introduce mechanical noises into the recording.

Outdoors, wind against the microphone will be very disturbing. It will be heard as a rumbling accompanied by a popping noise. Buy a wind shield with the microphone—or make one from foam rubber designed for acoustics—and use it when this occurs.

the soundman's job

The basic task of the soundman is to record the sound that goes with the picture. When filming, he records what the camera sees. In addition, he must supply the editor with the sound effects and ambience that are peculiar to the filmed location. He must always be listening for interesting sounds which give a location character, whether or not they have a direct relationship to what is being filmed. The more creative options he gives the editor, the better the film will be.

The soundman must always record the "presence" of a location. That is, he must make a recording of the natural sound which is present when dialogue and action are absent. If the location is a room, the presence is called "room tone." While it is sometimes difficult to keep the other production members quiet, he must tape as long a take as possible so that the editor can be selective.

When recording background sound, takes of several minutes are the most useful. The soundman must always be on the lookout for any local sounds that are unique or indigenous to the location, such

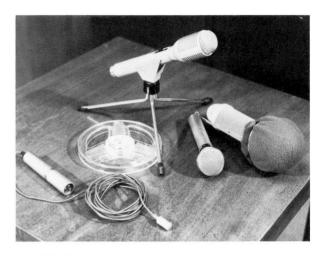

(*Photo* 78) Three microphones. In foreground, the tiny microphone is a Sony lavalier with the large Canon connector enclosing battery and preamplifier attached to the other end of the cable. On the stand is an Electrovoice omnidirectional condensor microphone. On the right is the AKG cardioid dynamic microphone beside its windscreen.

as traffic, animals, music or anything pictured in the film. If these effects are not recorded on location and are desired later, you will have to go to much trouble locating them in a sound-effects library.

summary

Involving the audience in time and place, giving the picture continuity and creating dramatic emphasis are the important functions that sound will serve in your film. Sound can also be used as a theme or as a symbol. Its creative potential is much greater than recording simple dialogue.

You will be recording your sound on a portable 1/4-inch tape recorder. The quality of your recording will depend mainly on whether you have set the volume control for the correct modulation and the manner in which you have placed the person speaking and the microphone. Background noise, boominess and sibilance are conditions to avoid when recording the human voice. When recording sound effects, special care must be taken with sounds which are especially sharp, soft or loud. Avoid handling the microphone during recording and have a wind shield handy when you are working outdoors. Record the presence or room tone of the location you are filming, as well as interesting local sounds and ambience. Above all, record longer takes than you think will be necessary so that the editor can be selective.

9. ANIMATION: THE INANIMATE COMES ALIVE

continuous filming • single-frame technique • the time-capsule film • three-dimensional figures, cutouts, silhouettes and drawings • the animation camera • movement and single- and triple-frame animation • the group project

Animation means bringing life or giving motion to something which would otherwise be static. In film, we immediately think of the animated cartoon, but this is only one example. Any film technique which generates movement in static material is animation. In the simplest case, if we continue to film at 24 fps and pan the camera over an inanimate object, such as a photograph, we have given it motion.

continuous filming

Many films have been made by panning and zooming over two-dimensional material, such as illustrations, still photographs and paintings. Films on the works of famous painters or illustrated children's books are the best examples. Without reference to the three-dimensional world, it does not matter whether we say the camera or the illustration moved. The image on the screen moves in an informative voyage into the details of the art.

Animating in this fashion requires precise control by the cameraman. Skipping and jerky camera motions are all the more noticeable when static material is involved.

single-frame technique

The heart of creative animation, however, involves, not continuous photography but single-frame photography. In the beginning of this book, we described how a pack of cards with line drawings could be flipped through to give the illusion of motion. We created this effect by first drawing a gradually changing figure on each of the cards. Single-frame photography with a motion-picture camera allows us to stop after each frame to make a slight alteration or change in the inanimate world. If these changes follow a continuous form, like the stick figure on the pack of cards, the image when screened will appear to be in motion.

Some Super 8 and 16mm cameras permit the

exposure of a single frame at a time. The operation of the camera start button will expose a single frame and advance to the next, but no further, until the button is pressed again. The duration of the exposure is constant and bears no relationship to the speed at which the film is advanced.

Suppose you were to place such a camera on a tripod on a street corner, lock the camera into position, then release the single-frame lever at different rates—once every second, then once every few seconds. When the film is screened, the street and the buildings will remain stationary, but the apparently still figures seated on park benches and the leaves on the trees will appear to be in a state of great agitation. People walking on the sidewalk will disappear out of the frame in a split second, and cars from the street in even less time. The effect is much the same as time-lapse photography which was discussed earlier.

When the camera is turned to inanimate material, the effect depends on what we do. We have already noted how we could pan and zoom over illustrations while continuously filming. With the single-frame release, we can pan and zoom in on a detail with absolute precision in a split second by first accurately planning the path of the movement, then by moving the camera and zoom bit by bit along the path after each frame of exposure. The precision of the screened effect would be impossible to achieve were the camera to run continuously.

the time-capsule film

A time-capsule film runs through hundreds of photographs, illustrations and newspaper clippings— related to an organization's growth, for example—

in a matter of minutes. This is usually done by focusing on each piece of material for only seconds or a fraction of a second if there is no zoom or panning movement. The rapid cutting and camera movements are timed to the rhythm of the music on the sound track. The result is a dazzling choreography of moving images on the screen. Only by first analyzing the movements frame by frame, then photographing the two-dimensional material with a single-frame release mechanism, has this result been possible.

An excellent example of this technique is the film *American Time Capsule**, which is a breathtaking history of the United States in three minutes. Another example is an animated film, a study of twenty-four hours of television by shooting a few frames for each new shot on television.

three-dimensional figures

Early animated films amazed audiences when familiar objects such as knives and forks appeared to move about and function by their own will, without any human intervention. The mysterious process by which these objects moved was based on single-frame photography. After each frame was exposed, the position of the object was slightly changed according to a preconceived pattern of movement; then the next frame was shot. In this way, the knife could appear to cut without the assistance of the human hand.

Another technique evolved around the use of clay. Beginning with a formless blob of clay, any type of figure and any number of figures could

*Distributed by Pyramid Films, Santa Monica, California

evolve by using the single-frame technique. After each frame of exposure, the filmmaker's fingers could alter the shape of the clay ever so slightly according to any form which struck his fancy. In the same way, pieces of clay could be separated from the main form and evolve into their own figures.

A good example of this genre is a film titled *Clay (Origin of the Species)*.* Made by a young film student at Harvard, *Clay* has won many awards and has been phenomenally successful in 16mm distribution.

cutouts and silhouettes

A different approach to animation uses cutout figures pressed flat against a shooting board by a piece of glass. For a silhouette effect, they can be pressed between two pieces of glass and positioned in front of an evenly lit background. Cutouts, however, have certain immediate limitations. For an arm to move, for example, either an entire new figure must be cut for each new frame or every few frames of exposure, or the arm can be hinged and made to move separately. Even with all the limbs hinged to move in any desired fashion, the movement will still appear stiff since there is no way of dealing with perspective.

The appearance of real motion may not, however, be the only objective. Cutout magazine photographs and illustrations can be amusingly juxtaposed in the kind of animated film where the

*Distributed by Contemporary Films/McGraw-Hill, New York, N.Y.

Eliot Noyes, Jr.'s *Clay (Origin of the Species)*, courtesy of Contemporary Films/McGraw-Hill

(*Photo* 79) A form of animation, effectively used by filmmakers of all ages, consists of a sequence of gradually changing clay objects.

change in imagery is more important than the movement of the forms themselves. Cutout figures can be placed against cutout backgrounds. A gorilla can suddenly be the featured guest at a backyard barbecue. Faces familiar from media coverage can say absurd things to each other by the simple insertion of cartoon dialogue. If the change of cutouts is quick and amusing enough, no one will miss the illusion of real motion.

drawings

Drawings are the basis of the cartoon, the most familiar animation technique. In its simplest form, a new drawing is made for every few frames of exposure, showing the figure as it evolves through a pattern of change. Chalk or grease pencils can be used on paper or surfaces which are erasable. More complex animation utilizes drawings on several layers of acetate which can be seen together against a background.

Take, for example, the line that moves mysteriously across a map and traces the course of an expedition. First, the map is laid flat across an animation board. Then a sheet of clear acetate is placed on top of the map, and the line is drawn in tiny sections every few frames across the acetate. Each shot will show the line to be just a bit longer and, when projected at normal speed, the line will appear to grow smoothly at the speed desired.

Several sheets of acetate may be involved if the action is more complex. For example, a figure appears against a background. If the drawings of the figure are made on a single sheet of acetate, the background will remain unchanged. If a second

Dusan Vukotic's *Ersatz*, courtesy of Contemporary Films/McGraw-Hill

(*Photo* 80) One of the easiest kinds of animation is a series of simple line drawings.

figure appears while the first figure remains still, a second layer of acetate can be used, leaving the background and the first figure unchanged. If the first figure is then required to move, only the first layer of acetate need be changed. This process is generally referred to as cell animation. Each sheet of acetate is called a cell, and the cells are changed for each frame of exposure as the action dictates.

the animation camera

For simple exercises in animation, such as the one outlined at the end of this chapter, any Super 8 or 16mm camera with a single-frame mechanism will be sufficient when securely mounted on a tripod or similar support. The professional animation unit consists of a camera and an elaborate support-and-table system. The camera support is mounted on the wall, and the camera is suspended over the animation table so that it can be raised or lowered by a pulley system. When the camera is lowered for each frame of exposure, the screen image will appear to zoom in. When it is raised, the image will zoom out.

The table itself moves horizontally in any direction by the operation of two hand-cranks. This allows for a panning movement in any direction across the cell; that is, the table moves in relation to the camera and not the other way around. The cells are placed over registration pins on the table so that the exact same placement can be guaranteed for each cell every time it is used.

movement and single- and triple-frame animation

Every animation camera operates a single frame at a time. The number of frames exposed for each cell depends on the character of the motion. For the smoothest motion, a change should be made for each frame of exposure, or a new cell should be drawn for every frame, or 24 drawings for each second of 16mm screen time. This would mean drawing 1440 different pictures for each *minute* of film. However, for the purpose of simple animation exercises, one drawing for every two or three frames of exposure should be sufficient.

Much depends on how quickly you want the figures to move and what illusion of speed you want to give them. For example, the roadrunner moves a great distance in the space of a few frames. His initial and final positions can be accurately drawn and the intervening frames represented by the progress of a few blurred lines. Similarly, a dog scratching can be represented by an accurate drawing of the foot in the upper and lower position with a few frames of blurred action in between. Most action can be adequately represented by a change in every two or three frames.

group project

For a group project, make a film one minute long on the meeting of an arrow and a circle. If there are twelve students in the group, let each one create a part or episode in the meeting lasting five seconds, or action which will be represented by forty drawings, i.e., 120 frames of exposure with a new drawing for every three frames of exposure.

First work out the episodes in the meeting and the outlines of the action by use of a storyboard. In order to keep the forms continuous from one drawing to the next, use tracing paper. Trace each drawing, then modify the form of the tracing and trace it out on the next drawing. If the drawings are of uniform size, then the forms will have a continuous relationship when animated.

When you shoot, don't change the position of the camera or the drawings. If you want the circle to come toward the screen, make a series of drawings in which the circle grows progressively larger.

Mount the camera on a tripod and point it either at the floor or a wall. Make sure the camera is at right angles to either surface and mark out a square the size of the drawing paper. Once the camera is in a position so that the square is just outside the edge of the frame-line in the viewer, lock it into position and tape the feet of the tripod. Now each drawing can simply be placed under and removed from the square.

Simple titles for your finished project may be created by either writing on a blackboard or lettering on paper, and shot with a camera mounted on a tripod or on an animation stand. They should be shot continuously at normal speed.

An alternative exercise would be to place the camera in front of a table top and use clay figures for the medium of change. Either method is simple to execute, and both amply illustrate the basis of creative animation: the single-frame technique.

10. EDITING: SHAPING THE FILM

---

the editing process: screening the rushes, cutting the assembly, the rough cut and the fine cut • the tools: the cutting table, the rewinds, the splicer and the viewer • the language of shots: synthesis, the narrative sequence and the montage • the feature and the documentary editor • cutting for continuity and discontinuity

Whether the film is narrative and has a story to tell, or documentary and seeks to relate an experience, or experimental, with a unifying idea, the job of the editor is to give that story, experience or idea its most powerful expression in terms of the shots he has been given. As we shall see in the next two chapters, his task goes far beyond splicing the tail of one shot onto the head of the next. Whether he is creating an entire event, putting together a montage or assembling a straightforward narrative sequence, his work must create a compelling rhythm in the flow of images. By pacing his cutting and controlling continuity, he can lead the audience to the heart of the film.

The first job of the editor is to meet with the director and project, or screen, the rushes. Once the footage has been shot, it is processed and duplicated onto a work print by the lab, and is called the rushes, or dailies. During the screening of the rushes, the work print will be run through several times and studied carefully. At this stage the first decisions will be made as to the exclusion of certain shots from the first assembly.

Constructing the first assembly is the second step the editor will take. This involves the grouping of shots or sequences together in an order which follows the script. The following are examples of considerations that should be taken into account when making the first assembly. If the first and the third sequences of a film were shot in the same location, while the second took place in another location, then sequences one and three will have been shot together and sequence two at another time. Also, the main action of a sequence may have been shot entirely before detail, reaction, and establishing shots. Shots focusing on a particular actor may also be grouped together for production economy.

The resultant lack of sequential form or order of the rushes is particularly true with documentary shooting, where the rushes may appear to follow no narrative thread whatsoever. For these reasons, the editor must first construct an assembly from the rushes that will follow as closely as possible, shot by shot, the sequential order of the final film as seen in the mind's eye. At this time, the editor should also remove the flash frames, the light or clear frames that occur in between shots.

When making up the assembly, the editor will also eliminate any material that he and the director had decided against using at the screening of the rushes. Usually, the shots eliminated at this stage will be those which are obvious mistakes: footage that is badly exposed, focused or composed; shots in which the camera movement is not satisfactory; and dramatic takes that were cut short because lines were muffed or the action miscued. In a feature film, generally only the best takes will have been printed.

Once the assembly is constructed, it, too, will be screened and screened again. The director and the editor must evaluate each shot against the intentions of the film as well as the effect of each take of a scene against other takes of the same scene. Once these evaluations have been made, the editor will continue to view the rushes until he can recall at will the subtlest details of each shot. It is important for the editor to have the shots well established in his mind at this point; otherwise, it will be difficult for him to envision his options when he becomes embedded in the detail of cutting.

The work of the editor is often referred to as "cutting." Not only does he make a physical cut in the film, but when he puts two shots together, he creates a "cut" in the film. When he creates a cut in a sequence, he must do it in such a way that the shots flow together with a sense of continuity. His business, then, is to ensure the film's continuity of space, time and motion.

The first attempt he makes to shape the individual shots into flowing, continuous sequences is .called the rough cut. This will then be reviewed with the director before the editor proceeds to make refinements in assembling a fine cut. In a professional film, the fine cut is not called the final cut until everyone, including the producer and the sponsor, is satisfied.

(*Photo* 81) The editing room: Moviola (left), film bins behind it for hanging shots in groups according to sequence, editing bench (right)

the tools: the cutting table, the rewinds, the splicer and the viewer

The process of cutting the picture, or the film stock, is a relatively simple matter in terms of mechanics. In addition to a projector, you need only an editing, or cutting, table equipped with a pair of rewind arms, a splicer, and a film viewer. The cutting table itself can be any table that is large and sturdy enough to support the rewinds. A rewind is a device which holds a reel on a spindle and, by means of a hand-crank, allows you to wind film from one reel to another (see photo 81).

There should at least be three feet between the two rewinds, or enough space to work with a viewer and a splicer between them. The film will run directly between the rewinds and can be wound in either direction by turning one or the other of the hand-cranks. The viewer is placed in the middle between the two rewinds and the film is threaded through it. In this way, a shot can be viewed over and over again at any speed and stopped at any frame for detailed analysis.

If your reel of film is "heads out," or with the beginning shot first, put the reel on the left rewind and wind from left to right. If it is "tails out," or with the closing shot first, put the reel on the right rewind and wind from right to left. This way, the image will always be right side up in the viewer. These rules will also apply when working with sound (chapter 11).

In addition to the rewinds, a professional editing

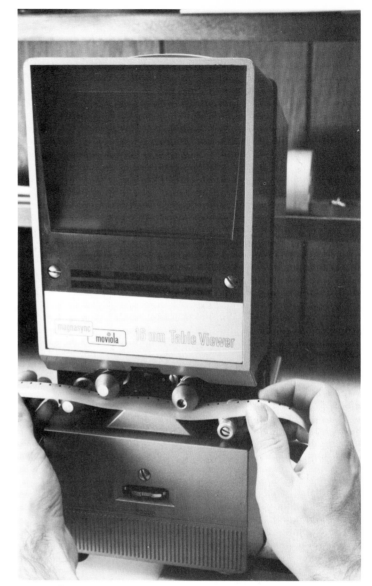

(*Photos* 82, 83) Threading the viewer (left). White leader is used for illustration. In a simple editing setup (right), the viewer may be used instead of a Moviola.

table should have a rack at the back for holding the editor's paraphernalia and film, and a frosted glass plate in the middle of the top, lit by a bulb from underneath, for reading edge numbers and the easy identification of any small piece of film.

The film viewer has a small screen and is easily threaded (see photos 82, 83) by slipping the film under a small pressure plate and around two or three guide wheels. It is operated by switching on the viewer light and cranking the film through on the rewinds.

There are no loops to form and no intermittent movement in this process. The image on the viewer screen is formed by means of a rotating prism which turns as the film advances. A certain amount of sharpness and steadiness is lost in the quality of the screened image. For this reason, the quality of focus and camera movements must initially be critically judged on the projector.

By studying a shot in the viewer, you can choose a particular frame at which you want to cut to the next shot. Stop the film in the viewer and mark that particular frame with a grease pencil. (Grease pencils are used since the mark can easily be erased with a piece of cloth or a cotton editor's glove.) Then find the frame to which you will cut on the following shot. Once you have marked this as well, you are ready to make a splice.

Splices were once made by cutting the two marked frames so that they overlapped slightly, then binding the overlap together with film cement. When two frames overlap, the base side of one contacts the emulsion side of the other. Since the emulsion, or dull side, cannot be cemented, it must first be scraped off along the edge of the overlap with a scraper or razor blade until all traces of the image have disappeared. Be thorough enough to scrape away all the emulsion, but careful enough not to scrape through and tear the base. With the

shot clamped in the splicer, a guide prevents scraping in the area of the next frame.

A thin application of film cement is then made on the area of overlap, and the base side of the second shot, also clamped in place in the splicer, is lowered into position and pressed firmly against the application of film cement. The splice is allowed to dry thoroughly before it is taken out of the splicer. Experimentation will tell you how long this takes; usually wait about twenty seconds.

A "hot splicer" has a heated base-plate to speed up the drying process. It also incorporates its own scraper which, in some models, is automatic (see photo 84). Cement splicing takes some amount of skill and patience and, fortunately, has been largely replaced in the editing room by the use of transparent Mylar tape. However, cement splicing is still used in preparing the original for printing (chapter 12).

Cement splicers cut slightly into the next frame for the area of overlap and, once a cut has been made, this frame is lost. You may want to try a cut several different ways, and the number of frames you would lose is a severe drawback to the cement splicing system.

With the exception of splicing original stock for laboratory printing, Mylar tape has almost totally replaced cement splicing within the past few years. Mylar splicers cut exactly between the frames, so that a frame is never lost. The two frames are joined together not by means of an overlap, but end to end with a piece of transparent tape over the top. (See photos 85, 86.)

For cutting, the film is held precisely on the splicer by registration pins through the sprocket holes. The piece of splicing tape, approximately three frames long, has its own sprocket holes, and these are placed over two registration pins in the area of the cut. For editing purposes, it is only

(*Photo* 84) A hot splicer is used to splice original to black leader with cement.

necessary to put tape on the emulsion side of the cut, though many editors prefer to tape both sides.

Super 8 editors usually combine the viewer with the rewinds on a small stand that can be placed on a desk or any table top (see photo 87). Mylar splicing tape for Super 8 is precut to the size of the splice. Precut tape can also be purchased for 16mm work, though generally a 66-foot roll is used and cut by hand.

Once you have put a sequence together in this fashion, screen your work on the projector. You will invariably find that there is some adjustment to make, and then it is back to the editing table. No matter how complex, there is no picture-editing trick or technique that can't be tried by using the process described above. The mechanical tools are simple, and your skill will increase with the trial-and-error method that is really the only way to learn the editing process.

You may also cut the picture on a machine called a Moviola or on recently introduced motorized editing tables, such as the models manufactured by KEM or Steenbeck. These machines mechanize the movement of the film through the viewing system, driving it either at the constant sound speed of 24 fps, or at variable speeds.

In professional editing, the Moviola was the standard piece of editing equipment until the mid-sixties, when the more versatile editing tables made their debut. It should be emphasized that they are not a necessary tool for editing, but are designed primarily for playing sound with picture in the editing process (chapter 11).

(*Photos* 85, 86) Making a splice in work print with transparent Mylar tape (top). The completed splice (bottom)

the language of shots: synthesis

The joining together of two or more shots creates a meaning that exists in none of the shots alone. This is synthesis. The simplest narrative sequence has been described as a shot of someone looking at something, a shot of what the person is looking at, and a third shot of the person's reaction to what he has seen. The second shot is known as the "point-of-view" (POV) shot, or "subjective camera" shot, and the third shot the reaction shot. It has been known since early editing experiments that the first and third shots can be identical, and yet the audience will interpret the expression of the person in the third shot according to what he has seen in the second shot: sad, if what he was looking at were a funeral; hungry, if it were food, etc.

Shots need not even relate to the same location for the coupling of shots to create a new meaning. Consider a shot of a mother nursing a baby secure in some nursery. Follow this by an exterior shot of speeding fire engines or police cars; then return in the third shot to the mother and baby. The nursery is no longer the secure place it was in the first shot, and we are concerned for the safety of the mother and baby. In fact, their security was already affected as soon as we saw the second shot. This is how film creates meaning. A shot works backward and forward in affecting the way we interpret other shots in a sequence.

(*Photo* 87) A Super 8 editor consisting of a viewer with rewinds

the narrative sequence
and the montage

The narrative sequence unites character, space and time in a storytelling manner. On the other hand, the montage, which is also a sequence of shots, is threaded together only by a central idea and knows no boundaries as to time, space or character.

In the opening montage of *North from Mexico*, one of the film scripts referred to in chapter 2, the sequence is made up entirely of shots of faces of Mexican-Americans in different locations. The idea is that, for them, the times are changing. We see pressed and energetic faces in an urban background, we see protest marchers, we see people at work in a field, irrigating according to age-old methods, and student politicians active in their university headquarters.

The shots of faces combine with the narration to synthesize the idea that times are changing. For the editor, the montage provides perhaps the most creative challenge that he will find in his work. However, as is particularly the case with the feature editor, his main concerns will be the continuity of film time and space, and the pacing of the progression of events.

the feature editor

The dramatic continuity is given to the editor by the script and the director's intentions. His job is to maintain this continuity by preventing the audience from becoming disoriented, and to enhance the drama by controlling the pace of the sequences. He helps maintain continuity by observing the axis of action just as the director did in shooting, and by making sure that the shots flow together within a sequence. In the matter of pacing, he has more creative latitude. He has to determine which details and cutaways will be inserted into the main course of action.

We have already seen how cutting to the comic's look of satisfaction allowed the dog to eat a whole pie in a few seconds. This use of a reaction shot allows us to shorten real time. Likewise, details can be added to lengthen the course of action and draw out suspense. If time should seem interminable as we await the execution of the prisoner with his head on the block, we can increase the tension by prolonging the observation of the expressions on the spectators' faces.

The rhythm of the cutting also affects the pacing of an event. Cutting quickly from shot to shot in a sequence can heighten the sense of action, while fixing on a scene with a single shot can seem endless.

the documentary editor

The task of the documentary editor is more complex. Generally, he is not given any dramatic continuity to follow in the usual sense. Often he must give shape to an entire event and, in doing so, he alone creates its time, space and character. Take, for example, the celebration of a national holiday at which brass bands and soldiers pass before a reviewing stand where dignitaries await the beginning of a ceremony. All of this is viewed by thousands of onlookers.

The event itself may take several hours, and one or several cameramen may record the processions and ceremony from numerous vantage points. With the hundreds of shots that the editor reviews, he may be required to re-create the event in only minutes of film time. The shots he chooses will give the character, size and pacing of the event to the audience, for they will have no other vantage point.

Assuming the cameramen have provided the appropriate material, he can open up the event to the audience by combining sweeping long shots with detailed material from different points of view. In this way, film can heighten the sense of an event by magically transporting the audience to different vantage points that would otherwise be unavailable to the spectator.

By cutting together the different perspectives with the reactions of the participants and onlookers, he can successfully compress the duration of the event while still preserving its integrity. Even though the event takes only several minutes of screen time, if the editor's coverage has been complete, the audience will not experience a truncation of the event but will relate the few minutes on film to a much broader span of time in their imaginations.

By the editor's selection of expressions of the participants, dignitaries and onlookers, he can create the atmosphere and character of the event. Pious dignitaries and humble onlookers will create a considerably different impression of the event selection, therefore, the editor must be careful to try to re-create the real character of the event.

By careful design—as, for example, in Leni Riefenstahl's *Triumph of the Will*—the filmmaker can create or emphasize a very special mood. This is why film can be such a potent instrument of propaganda.

cutting for continuity

In the chapter on shooting, we discussed filming the same scene from two different perspectives so that the action would overlap. The reason for this overlap is to allow the editor to choose a cutting point which will be best for the timing of the scene.

When we cut on a continuous action from one perspective to another, we must be sure that every element of the action in the first shot at the moment of the cut is duplicated in the second. This is called match cutting.

If comic B had his hand over his heart in the first shot and over his mouth in the second at the point of the cut, there would be a mismatch of an important element, and the audience would experience a lapse in continuity. If the action of comic A were sufficiently absorbing, the audience might not have been aware of the position of B's hand in the

(*Photos* 88, 89, 90) When cutting for continuity, the axis of action must be maintained. If we cut from the medium shot to the close-up below it, the second shot will appear to be a third person and not the man at the table since we do not expect to see him from this angle. The correct cut would be from the medium shot to the close-up (bottom).

first shot, and we would be able to get away with the mismatch. This would be a case of the sleight of hand that so often comes into play in editing.

Besides the position of hands and head (comic B cannot be looking down in the first shot and up in the second), other important elements which can be mismatched include wardrobe articles and the placement of props: an open jacket must remain open; a small radio seen in the first shot cannot suddenly disappear in the second. In a large production, one person is usually assigned the task of checking the continuity of these elements during the shooting.

Motion begun in one shot should, in general, continue through the succeeding shots until it has come to rest. If our subject is in motion at the cutting point of the first shot, he must continue to be in motion in the second. If the camera is in motion at the cutting point in the first shot, it must continue in a similar motion in the second. A pan can be cut to a second pan if it is going in the same direction and at the same speed. Sometimes a pan can be cut into the motion of a dolly shot, but cutting to the movement of a zoom will hardly ever work.

If we have a combination of subject movement and camera movement, we will be able to cut to a static shot if the subject movement continues and is sufficiently distracting. For example, if we are panning with the movement of the parade in a long shot, we can cut to a close static shot of the band passing in front of the camera before the pan has come to rest. The eye does not perceive the discontinuity of camera movement because the movement of the subject in the second shot is so distracting. This is another case of the editor indulging in a sleight of hand. The eye is attracted to one thing so it does not see another.

In fact, the editor can get away with a great deal if

(*Photos* 91, 92) Match cutting. A cut from the medium shot (top) to the close-up (bottom) will disrupt attention because the girl's hand will appear to jump from the table to her face.

he keeps the eye interested. Suppose we are watching a couple approaching from a street corner. If they are attractive and absorb our interest, we will want to see them come close to the camera and perhaps follow them. But suppose the course of the film cannot allow us to linger and must disappoint our anticipations. If the couple momentarily disappears from sight because a car passes in front of them, we may choose this exact moment to cut to another element of the street corner scene. The couple did not have to walk out of the frame since the passing car provided a distraction sufficient to pass us onto the next shot without a sense of discontinuity. Like the magician's handkerchief, the car distracts the eye and unveils a new shot.

In every shot, the eye finds a center of attention. When cutting for continuity, we can change the shot, but we should always maintain the center of attention. If the couple approaches moving into the center of the frame, we should cut to someone moving likewise in the center of the frame. The immediate replacement of the center of attention distracts the eye from the cut. If the action causes us to look to the right side of the frame, then the insertion of a detail or reaction shot should not be one that dominates the left side of the frame. The eye needs instant gratification; otherwise, it senses a jump in the cut.

When we cut from long shot to medium shot and from medium shot to a close-up, our attention is drawn to detail, and we welcome the shift in perspective. When we cut from close-up detail to close-up, the frame is filled with and our attention occupied by recognizable objects. But cutting from medium shot to medium shot does not often work easily, and it is almost impossible to cut successfully from long shot to long shot. There is too much room in the frame over which our attention can wander, and we quickly become aware of graphic

(*Photos* 93, 94) Costume mismatch. We cannot cut from the medium shot above to the close-up below since the girl has zipped her jacket to the neck. This kind of inconsistency can easily occur if the director or editor does not keep a sharp eye on details. The viewer would be disoriented by the mismatched cut.

dissimilarities. When the cut comes we experience a jump.

In experimenting with two shots in order to find the smoothest cutting point, it sometimes helps to stop the film in the viewer at a cutting point and, with a grease pencil, trace the center of attention and the graphic outline of the frame on the glass screen of the viewer. Then move to a cutting point in the beginning of the second shot and compare the graphic balance as well as the new center of attention. If there is a sufficient shift in either, this may result in a distracting jump when the film is projected on a screen.

If the location remains constant within a sequence, a change of lighting may cause discontinuity. Changes in exposure from shot to shot will be distracting but, if not too great, these can be evened out in the final answer print (chapter 12). There is, however, no satisfactory way of dealing with changes in lighting quality. In an exterior scene, the lighting may go from sharp to soft if the sun goes behind a cloud in between shots. When the shots are cut together, it will seem like a change in location.

cutting for discontinuity

The very jump that is distracting in a narrative sequence may be used to positive and amusing effect in a film that is cut to the rhythm of music on the sound track. For example, graphic forms or figures can be made to jump from one side of the screen to the other in time with the rhythm. The jumping is no longer a distraction, but the very statement of a rhythmic theme.

Discontinuity is often referred to as jump cutting.

In general, this occurs when the audience is not prepared for a change within a scene or a change from scene to scene. In the past, lap dissolves (where the end of one shot dissolves into the beginning of the next) and fades (where the shot fades in or out from the image to blackness) have been used to prepare the audience for a significant change in time or location.

These devices, however, are being used less and less, and films are now relying more and more on the straight cut. Audience sophistication has grown and, in most cases, dramatic preparation is sufficient. We expect to cut to the next scene when we feel the present scene has been effectively concluded. If we cut away from the scene when the audience does not expect it, we may do so intentionally in order to introduce an element of surprise or spontaneity.

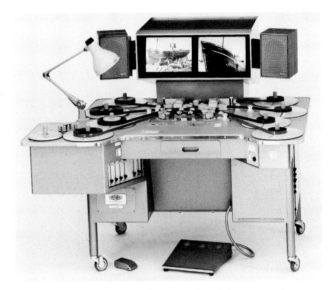

(*Photo* 95) The Steenbeck editing console

summary

After viewing the rushes, the editor's job begins with the creation of the film assembly. To do this, he eliminates shots which did not turn out well and arranges the remainder in an order which resembles as closely as possible the order of shots in the film-to-be. His first attempt to cut the shots into flowing sequences is called the rough cut. The editing then progresses to its final stage with the fine cut.

In order to cut the picture, the tools he needs are relatively simple: a projector, a cutting table with rewinds, a film viewer and a splicer. With these tools he can perfect his cutting through trial and error, whether he is working on a straightforward narrative sequence or the complex effects of a montage.

Meaning in a film is created by the synthesis of shots: one shot affects the way we interpret other shots in a sequence. Within a sequence, both documentary and feature editor are concerned with the continuity of space, time and motion. The feature editor, in particular, is concerned with how the details of a sequence affect its pacing. The documentary editor is not presented with any dramatic continuity to uphold, and must often give shape to entire events by his cutting alone.

Cutting for continuity concerns many factors. Cutting on action requires the careful matching of shots. Movement begun in one shot, whether by subject or camera, must continue through the next until it has come to rest. A moving shot can be cut to a static one only if the subject movement is sufficiently distracting. Above all, the editor must be aware of the eye's center of attention when cutting from shot to shot within a sequence.

11. THE SOUND TRACK: THE PICTURE SPEAKS

Super 8 sound: striping and double-system • 16mm sound • sound transfer • the synchronizer • the moviola • coding • splicing magnetic stock • editing sync sound • room tone • building the music and effects tracks

super 8: the magnetic stripe

Super 8 as an amateur medium has made only limited use of sound until fairly recently. Magnetic striping is the most common way of adding sound to a Super 8 film. After you have edited the picture, you can have a magnetic stripe printed along the edge of the film—out of the picture area—onto which you can record the sound track for your film. If you have a Super 8 sound projector, it will have some facility for recording sound from a tape recorder, microphone or record player directly onto the magnetic stripe.

Some Super 8 sound projectors are quite sophisticated in this respect. Some, such as the Bolex, will allow you to record music and then go back over the track again to record a voice-over narration which can be superimposed over the music. Others, such as the Eumig, will allow you to mix several sources of sound in one recording: for example, a microphone, tape recorder and record player may be mixed together through an input unit.

In all cases the recording technique is basically the same. The film is projected and, while you watch the screen, you add the appropriate sound at the precise time. The signal from the microphone, tape recorder or record player is fed by a cable into the input on the projector. Depending on the projector, there may or may not be a means of measuring the incoming signal. The projector may utilize either the indicator light or VU-meter measuring system described in chapter 7. There may even be an automatic level control.

Magnetic striping and recording by means of a projector works fairly well for a simple music track or voice-over narration, but its great limitation is that there is no way of linking sound to picture with frame-to-frame accuracy. Your sound may or may not begin and end when you want it to. There is no way of using synchronous dialogue, cutting to the rhythm of music or using sound effects with reasonable accuracy.

In order to synchronize dialogue or other sound in Super 8, you must begin with a Super 8 sync sound system as described in chapter 8. With these systems, the sound is first recorded by double-system on a tape recorder which runs in sync with the camera. It is then transferred either to magnetic sound stock identical in size and sprocket-hole pattern to Super 8 film, or to 16mm magnetic stock, and edited simultaneously with the picture. In this case, the editing procedure is the same as that for 16mm sync sound.

16mm sound

16mm film can likewise be striped and a simple music or voice-over narration track recorded. However, a more precise sound-editing technique is based upon the use of separate magnetic tracks, called double-system, which only at the final stage of film editing are transferred directly onto the film. As we shall see, the use of separate magnetic tracks during the editing process has the tremendous advantage of allowing you to lay in, or align, sound in a frame-to-frame relationship with the picture.

transferring from $\frac{1}{4}$-inch tape to magnetic stock

Sync sound is transferred to 16mm magnetic stock while the rushes are being processed. To do this, you take the $\frac{1}{4}$-inch tape to a sound lab, making sure that it is clearly marked "sync sound." As a very rough estimate, transferring will cost approximately one-third the cost of processing the original and making a work print for film of a similar duration.

In chapter 8, we discussed how a sync pulse is recorded on the $\frac{1}{4}$-inch tape and how this provides a record of the camera's speed. When the tape is transferred, two recording machines are involved: one to play back the $\frac{1}{4}$-inch tape and the other to re-record the signal on 16mm sprocketed magnetic sound stock. During the transfer, the sync pulse is "read" and, depending on the type of transfer system, the pulse controls the speed of either the $\frac{1}{4}$-inch machine or the 16mm transfer machine so that the speed of the camera motor is duplicated.

This ensures that the actual length of the 16mm magnetic stock onto which the sound is being transferred will be exactly the same length as the corresponding piece of film on which the picture is printed. Then, when the start mark on the 16mm magnetic sound track and the start mark on the picture are lined up, the two pieces of film will run in a frame-to-frame, precise synchronous relationship.

If you have access to a sync-sound recorder, such as the Nagra (photo 75), and a transfer recorder for 16mm magnetic stock, such as the small Magnasync (photo 96), you can do your own transfer work. All you need is a resolver, such as the Nagra's SLO unit, which will read the sync pulse on the tape and "slave," or precisely match, the Nagra's speed to the camera's.

Nonsync material (often referred to as wild sound), such as sound effects, music or separately recorded voice-over narration, does not require the use of a resolver and can be transferred on the Magnasync. Nonsync sound can also be transferred by using a single-system sound camera or a projector that is equipped to record on 16mm magnetic stock. In this case the magnetic stock is threaded as film would be, and the tape recorder sound output is fed into the sound input of the camera or projector.

In Super 8 sync sound, the MIT/Leacock system described in chapter 7 is sold with a resolver/transfer unit which re-records the sync sound from the cassette original onto Super 8 sprocketed magnetic stock. Super 8 Sound System, on the other hand, records directly on Super 8 magnetic

(*Photo* 96) The Magnasync 16mm transfer recorder

stock and there is no need to transfer. For the beginner, this saves a step, but the experienced filmmaker will not want to edit his original sound since restored cuts are not always satisfactory.

With the MIT/Leacock or the Beaulieu/Uher systems, the original sound along with a sync signal is on magnetic tape. It can therefore be transferred, if desired, to 16mm magnetic stock and edited on an editing console which takes Super 8 picture along with 16mm sound. This will give you the option of being able to use 16mm sound mixing facilities (see chapter 12).

After the rushes and the transferred sound material have been received, the editor must sync up all the sync-sound takes with the corresponding picture takes; that is, line up the picture and sound of each take so that they begin precisely at the same point. This can be accomplished by means of a synchronizer, or a sound-editing machine, such as the Moviola, KEM or Steenbeck mentioned in the previous chapter.

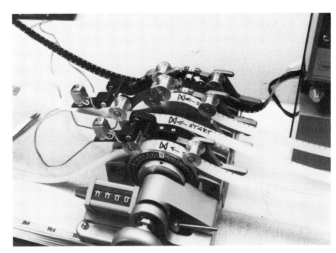

(*Photo* 97) Lining up sync start marks in the synchronizer: start marks on white leader for three sound tracks, and round punch mark on picture in fourth gang. Note open sound heads to left for two front gangs, footage counter set at 0000.

the synchronizer

The synchronizer is the simplest editing tool that keeps the picture in a frame-to-frame relation with anywhere from one to three sound tracks at a time. It consists of a central axle with from two to four fixed, sprocketed wheels (photo 97). The sprockets on the wheels match the sprocket holes in the film and the wheels move in a fixed relationship to one another. Each wheel and its film clamp is called a gang.

The start mark on the picture and the start mark on the magnetic track must be lined up with an indicator on the synchronizer. On the picture, the start mark is indicated either by the closing of the clapstick or a series of four "flashed" frames if the automatic marker system inside the camera is used. To find the sound of the clapstick closing on the sound track, you must read the sound with a magnetic head and sound amplifier.

The magnetic head can be attached to one of the gangs on the synchronizer and the signal fed into a small amplifier with a speaker (photo 97). A sound reader which is separate from the synchronizer may be used instead. If the automatic marker has been used, there will be an identifying beep of a few frames in length on the sound track. If the clapstick was used, a "clack" can be found occupying a single frame after the soundman's verbal slate, or his announcement of the scene and the take number.

Once the two start marks are lined up, the picture and sound track can be run through the synchronizer together and marked off at the end of each take. Do not use a grease pencil to mark the magnetic sound track as the grease will collect on the playback heads and affect reproduction. Use a quick-drying felt-tip pen, writing on the shiny side of the stock or on the dull side near the sprocket holes (since the sound is recorded only on the edge of the 16mm mag stock, away from the sprockets). Writing on the recorded area will mar the quality of the sound.

When lining up sync takes in this manner, always do your splicing to the left of the synchronizer. This will ensure that everything to the right of the synchronizer, or the takes you have already synced up, will remain in sync.

(*Photo* 98) Marking 16mm magnetic stock on the oxide (dull) side, next to the sprocket holes and not on the other edge

the moviola

In place of the synchronizer, a Moviola can be used to sync up the rushes. When using the sound reader, or head, on the synchronizer, the track is driven by the rewinds. Because it is very difficult to keep the speed of your winding constant, i.e., 24 fps, the quality of the sound reproduction will be poor at best. The Moviola (photo 81) is driven at constant or variable speed by an electric motor. For matching sound to picture, the constant speed of the sound motor drive permits a much higher quality of sound reproduction.

When cutting sync sound on the Moviola, a simple procedure is to mark the beginning and end frames of each cut on the picture and the corresponding sections on the sound tracks, then rewind, or reverse, the sections toward the feed reels (see photo 99). If the Moviola is placed with feed reels near an editing table, the cuts and splices can be made without having to take the film off the Moviola. By always reversing the area to be cut and working off the feed reels, the footage that is already on the take-up reels will remain in sync. This is an application of the same principle as always working to the left of the synchronizer.

The KEM and Steenbeck editing consoles mentioned in chapter 10 function in much the same way as the Moviola. Editing consoles, which cost three times as much as upright Moviolas, are used only by established professionals.

For Super 8 sound editing, there are editing tables available which use a constant-speed motorized drive for the synchronizer. Some consoles (the MIT/Leacock system) synchronize Super 8 film

(*Photo* 99) Moviola, with film bin in left background. Picture is on right reel, sound on left. Feed reels are in back, take-up reels in front.

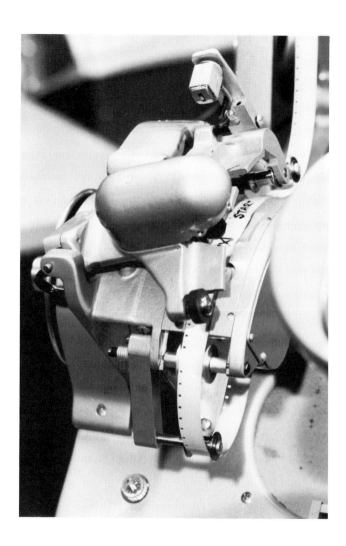

(*Photos* 1·00, 101) Threading of picture in Moviola with gate open (left). Note punch mark in gate. Threading head leader of magnetic track in sound section of Mov-iola (right). When sound head (shown lifted) is dropped into place, it will just cover sync start mark.

with Super 8 magnetic stock, while others (the Handiola) link the Super 8 picture frame-by-frame with 16mm magnetic stock.

coding

Once all the sync sound takes have been lined up and linked together in this fashion, they are ready to be coded. When a small piece of film falls on the cutting-room floor, it can easily be identified by looking at it against a light; but when a piece of magnetic track is misplaced, there is nothing to see on the magnetic oxide, and a short section of track is difficult to read on a sound reader. For this reason, synced-up and assembled track and picture are given an identical series of numbers which are printed along the sprocketed edge. Since coding is such a time-saver, it is an automatic step in professional work.

splicing magnetic stock

Just like film, magnetic stock has a base side which is shiny. The other side is dull and is coated with iron oxide for recording sound. Splices are bound with white, perforated Mylar tape which is always placed on the base side—never on the oxide side.

Splicers for magnetic stock are unlike those for film tape splices, in that the cutting elements are made from an alloy to prevent the oxide from becoming magnetized by the cut. If this were to happen, you would introduce a "click" onto your sound track.

Alloy splicers either make a straight cut, which corresponds to the frame line on the picture, or a diagonal cut. Even with an alloy cutter, a straight splice may introduce a "click." This is because the slightest separation of the stock at the point of the splice can read like a click to the playback head. The diagonal splice is designed to eliminate this possibility. However, straight cuts made on a high-quality magnetic-stock splicer will usually not suffer this defect, and in addition, this type of splicer can be used to cut the picture.

The beginner can equip a modest 16mm editing room with a pair of rewinds ($60), a splicer (from $25-$135) and a viewer (from $195-$325). An editing table (optional) with built-in light well will cost $150. Synchronizers will run from $110-$200, depending upon the number of gangs. Synchronizers may be equipped with sound heads ($32) which require an amplifier ($64). The professional 16mm editing room will have a Moviola ($3,000). All the above equipment may be purchased secondhand

Super 8mm picture-editing equipment, made for mass marketing, is considerably cheaper. Super 8 editing equipment for double-system sound is comparable in price to 16mm.

editing sync sound

With a dramatic sync-sound take, the dialogue has been worked out in advance and the entire take will be used. It will begin and end with sufficient pause for pacing the cuts. A cut at the head of the take and one at the end may be all that is necessary, although the picture take may be cut to include a reaction shot or inserted detail.

The documentary sound take is usually preceded

by no such preparation, although the "setup" interview falls somewhere in between. When we are dealing with documentary dialogue, often much of what is said will not be included in the final film. If the shot is held constantly on someone speaking, we may want to cut out the middle portion of what he says.

First, we must find a sufficient pause in the dialogue to make the sound cut. There should be a few frames of silence after the last word before the cut and a slightly longer pause before the first word after the cut. If a new sentence begins after the cut, then a pause of 10 to 20 frames is necessary to make the sound cut seem natural. Too short a pause will make the cut sound choppy.

Once the sound cut has been made, the picture must be shortened as well. However, the picture cut, when viewed on the screen, will give an example of one of the least acceptable jump cuts: the head of the speaker shifts slightly and instantaneously at the moment of the cut.

What we need at this point is a cutaway on the picture reel and a return after a phrase or two to the main speaker. The cutaway can be to the interviewer, a listener or anyone who has been previously established in the film. Or it can cut to a series of shots related to what the speaker is talking about. Whatever length of picture we insert, we must take out an equivalent length of the speaker picture. Either of these solutions, the reaction shot or the cutaway series, will bridge the unwanted jump cut.

During a pause in the dialogue, an unintentional and distracting sound from the background or the speaker may occur: the banging of a door, an off-screen voice, or the rustle of clothing picked up by the speaker's microphone. If the room is otherwise quiet, our first impulse would be to take out this little piece of sound and replace it with a slug, or piece of leader or other blank film stock. What

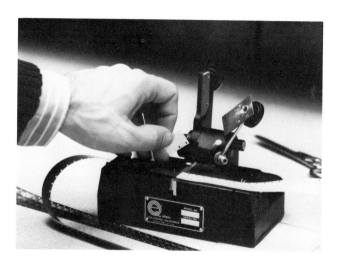

(*Photos* 102, 103) Splicing white leader to magnetic, sprocketed sound track (top). The completed splice (bottom). Splicing tape is always applied on the shiny (base) side, magnetic coating is on dull side.

happens is that when we play this back, we discover "room tone."

room tone

Room tone is the "sound" of the room in which we are recording. If the filming is done outside, this is often called "ambience," or simply "presence." Every room has its own acoustics, made up of everything from ventilation systems to the reverberations of background noise, and our hearing is subconsciously quite attuned to this sound. Remove it for only a moment, and we are very distracted by its absence on the sound track, which now registers absolute silence.

Absolute silence is very different from the normal sound of even an exceptionally quiet room. For this reason, the soundman should always make a separate recording of room tone or exterior ambience. This can then be plugged into the small cuts we may wish to make in the sound track. Another solution would be to take a cut from a pause in the dialogue in a portion of the take that you do not intend to use. This will also be your only alternative when no room tone has been recorded.

building the music and effects tracks

In the chapter on sound recording, we discussed the various uses of sound with film. In order to make full use of the creative potential of sound, we must usually build several sound tracks which would run simultaneously with the picture. When the fine cut of the picture is complete, these tracks are taken with the picture to the sound lab where they are "mixed" together to form a single sound track. The "mix" will be covered in the following chapter.

Going back to the scene of the mother and the child in the nursery, suppose the following: the mother is singing a lullaby; the sound of a radio comes from another room; an open window in the background of the shot allows us to hear fire engines passing on the street below; after the fire engines have passed, a telephone rings. Why couldn't we record all these sounds on one sync take?

The radio and the telephone would not be so difficult to arrange, but can you imagine cueing a fire engine with the action just to get the sound on the sync or dialogue track?

By recording these sounds separately, we can add them to the sync take of the lullaby at the editing stage by building additional tracks. Not only does this simplify production, but the mixer can then treat these sounds separately and give them just the right dramatic presence or volume during the mix. This also allows the director to change his mind about the effects and the editor to experiment with different effects in order to achieve the right dramatic balance.

Generally, you will record your own sound effects on a ¼-inch tape recorder and then transfer them to 16mm magnetic stock. Or you may find the sound effect you want on a sound-effects record or in the sound-effects library of a sound studio. For example, you would not want to re-create by yourself the sound of a giant explosion. Once the sound effect is re-recorded onto 16mm magnetic stock, you are ready to lay it in to correspond to the picture.

(*Photo* 104) Editing bench. Film and magnetic tracks coming off reels on left pass through four-gang synchronizer and viewer. Splicer and sound amplifier are in background.

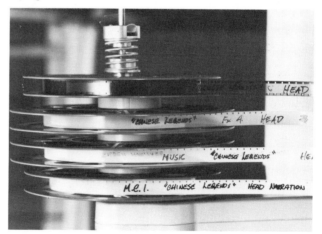

(*Photo* 105) Three sound tracks and work-print picture feeding off reels on rewind. Note how leaders are marked: *Chinese Legends* (title), Head Narration. Second is music; third, sound effects (abbreviated "FX A"). The reels are spaced to feed smoothly into synchronizer by placing plastic cores in between.

By using a synchronizer or a Moviola, you can build one sound track at a time against the picture. Make a mark on the magnetic sound track where the effect occurs: for example, place an X on the track by the frame where the telephone begins to ring and where it ends. Now you can lay the effect in next to the appropriate frame of picture, lining up the track with the picture on a synchronizer or Moviola. Remember, work to the left of the synchronizer, then the work you have already completed will remain in the correct frame-to-frame relationship to the right of the synchronizer.

In the example of the mother and child, the sound of the radio will begin and end concurrently with the picture take. It will require a separate track that we can call FX A (FX stands for sound effects). The sound of the fire engines occurs concurrently with the radio so that it, too, will require a separate track, called FX B. This sound effect comes in at a specific time and we hear nothing else from this track until that time. Therefore, until the time of the sound effect, we build this track with "fill" and splice the fire-engine sound onto the fill at the appropriate frame.

Fill is nonmagnetic spacer and can be anything from unused work print to opaque film stock sold for this purpose. There are two things to remember when using fill. First, the shiny, or base, side of film fill should always be spliced on the same side as the oxide side of the magnetic track. This is because the emulsion, or dull, side of the fill can rub off on the reproduction heads during editing or at the studio at the time of the mix. Second, the magnetic stock has sprocket holes on only one side. Use single-perf fill so that this is kept uniform. If you use double-perf fill, you may accidently put a piece of track in the wrong way and ruin the sound side in the editing machines.

After the fire-engine sound has continued long

enough to be gradually faded out (fading is done at the time of the mix), continue the track by adding on another piece of fill. The next sound is the ringing of the telephone. If there are a few feet of silence after the fire engines have faded out before the telephone rings, you can also put this effect on FX B.

The space between the fire engines and telephone is important for the following reason: after the mixer has faded out the fire engines, he must wait till there is silence on the track—the silence provided by the nonmagnetic fill—before he can again turn up the volume control for the FX-B track. The volume must be up by the time the telephone is to ring. If there is not sufficient space for him to do this, the telephone ring should go on a separate track, which would be called FX C.

In general, when cutting voice-over dialogue or sound effects to picture, do not have a word or a short, loud noise coincide with a picture cut. This will emphasize the cut and make it look jumpy. Try to space dialogue so that a short pause falls over the cut. If a word must fall over the cut, words with vowels will work better than words with sharp consonants. Of course, if a cut is not supposed to be smooth but shocking or surprising, then you may want a sharp sound to fall over it.

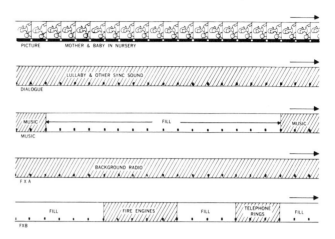

(*Fig.* 17) Four magnetic sound tracks aligned in a frame-to-frame (sync) relationship with the picture.

sound dissolves

One of the uses of theme music is to build a sound bridge from scene to scene. Suppose theme music introduces us to the above scene and comes in again at the end to take us to the next scene. The theme music will also require a separate track, which will be called MUSIC A. In the beginning of the scene, the music track will overlap with DIAL A and FX A for at least a few feet. This will allow the mixer time to fade-in the other sounds underneath the music in the beginning of the scene. There will be a similar overlap at the end of the scene, and DIAL A and FX A will be faded out as MUSIC A comes in. This is called a sound dissolve, or segue.

Sound dissolves can be made quickly. The timing of the dissolve depends on the kind of sound and the type of effect you want to create. However, a minimum of one-foot overlap is recommended in laying out your tracks.

cutting to music

Suppose you want to make a film with only music on the sound track. This is a good idea since it is simple. It will teach you a good deal about how sound affects picture and, as mentioned earlier, can be quite amusing when the picture is cut to the rhythm of the music. When cutting picture to music in this way, the music track is analyzed before the picture is edited beyond the assembly stage. Analyzing the music means simply marking out its rhythm and the progression of the passages on the track. Then, by using a synchronizer or Moviola, you can make picture cuts on the beat or a measure off the beat in a syncopated style.

If you plan a more complicated sound track, there are some general guidelines to follow. First, cut your picture with the dialogue track. Whether it is dramatic dialogue, a documentary interview or voice-over narration, the human voice will take precedence on your sound track. Then cut in the music if you plan to use any. Pauses or lapses in the dialogue track will usually be cues for the musical theme.

The best way to do this so that you can hear what you are doing is to use a Moviola equipped to run two sound tracks simultaneously. You can also do this with a three- or four-gang synchronizer with two magnetic heads. However, it is so difficult to discriminate between sounds with this system that it is often better to cut the second track separately and use the two heads only as a check.

Lastly, add the sound effects. Since either the dialogue or the music may affect the placement of the effect, you will have to check both, one at a time, against the sound-effects track. Not until the mix at the sound studio (see next chapter) will you have the opportunity to hear all your tracks together.

summary

Adding a magnetic stripe to the final cut of your picture provides a means of putting a simple narration or music sound track to your film. If you are working in Super 8, you will have to be content with this voice-over narration or musical accompaniment unless you have access to one of the Super 8 sync-sound systems, whereby you can link sound to picture with frame-to-frame accuracy.

Professional sound technique is based on transferring the recorded sound to sprocketed magnetic stock of the film gauge you are using, and locking the sound in a frame-to-frame relationship with the picture while you are editing with the use of a synchronizer or Moviola. The synchronizer is used in conjunction with rewinds and has a provision for mounting a magnetic head which can be used in conjunction with a small amplifier to read the sound.

A sound reader which is separate from the synchronizer but which combines the head and amplifier can also be used. The Moviola is a superior sound-editing system since it is driven by an electric motor with constant speed, permitting higher quality sound reproduction.

Magnetic stock is spliced by use of a special splicing black, and white perforated Mylar tape. The tape is always placed on the base side of the magnetic stock and the soft, dull or emulsion side of the fill.

The rushes are synced up on either the synchronizer or the Moviola by lining up the start mark on the picture with the start mark on the track. Dialogue sound deletions necessitate the use of cutaway material. Small cuts in the dialogue track can be filled with room tone or presence.

Music and sound effects are added to the dialogue by building separate music and effects tracks. When such a track has no sound on it, it is spaced by fill until the next sound comes along. In general, the dialogue or narration is cut to the picture, then the music is cut to the dialogue and picture, and finally, the effects are cut to the picture and whatever other sound is dominant. For all the tracks to be heard together with the picture, the sound is taken to the sound lab where the various tracks are mixed.

12. FINISHING THE FILM

marking the work print • titles and copyright • preparing for the mix • making a sound log • the mix • matching the original and cutting the a & b rolls • preparing printing leaders • the optical track • a & b rolls and release printing

marking the work print

When you are approaching the fine cut in 16mm or 35mm, and if you are going on to A & B roll printing (which will be explained later in this chapter), you will want to indicate on the work print where fades and dissolves (see glossary) will occur. These are two standard optical effects which are available at the lab when a final print of your film is made.

Some labs will print fades and dissolves of only one standard length. Others can offer a variety of lengths, such as 16, 24, 32, 64 and 96 frames, for each effect. Before marking out the length of the effect on the work print, consult with the lab you have chosen to work with. Figure 18 shows how to mark your work print to indicate where the effects will be.

Effects other than fades and dissolves are done in an optical printer. Optical printing is specialized, and you will have to go to an optical house for the service. The most common of these effects available for 16mm is the freeze frame. Other effects include the optical zoom, skip and multiple-frame printing techniques. These services are expensive and unless the effect is of crucial importance, think of a simpler way of achieving a similar result.

titles and copyright

Since titles are almost always accompanied by some sound, you must know how many you will have and where they will be before you can mix the sound. In the simplest film, there must be a main title and a title for production credits. In professional films, these are usually printed by a graphic artist and shot on an animation stand; but for a class exercise, they can be created simply by writing on a blackboard and filming with a camera mounted on a tripod. Prestype or Letraset-brand lettering (available at most art supply stores) offers another inexpensive, but more sophisticated means of designing the title material. If you use white lettering on opaque black paper, the lab can superimpose the title over a shot in your film by using a double-exposure technique. This service is standard with A & B roll printing.

If you believe that there is any possibility whatever of your film being used commercially—that is,

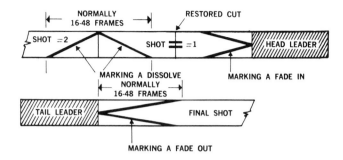

(*Fig.* 18) Marking the work print for projection and matching. The work print is marked with the above symbols for fade-ins, fade-outs and dissolves, showing the length of these effects to the negative cutter (the technician who cuts and matches the camera original to the work print). In addition, these markings provide the filmmaker with some visual indication of the effects during projection of the work print. Restored cuts: there will always be some shots which have been cut short and were later lengthened during the trial-and-error process of editing. The two parallel marks show the negative cutter that the splice does not indicate a new shot.

sold or rented for profit—then you will want to copyright it. This is a very simple procedure that begins with the title. The copyright symbol, which is a *c* in a small circle, is followed by the name, either individual or corporate, of the copyright holder, and the year of issue; e.g., © James Doe, 1976. This must be placed on or near the main title, and is usually written in smaller type than the film credits.

After you have made several prints of your film, if you are willing to spend the money, you will send two copies of it along with a form and a small fee, to the Library of Congress in Washington, D.C. For the exact details, write to the Library of Congress and they will mail you all the necessary instructions and forms.

Should you fail to send your two prints, fee and form to Washington, do remember to include the © James Doe, 1976, on the film; then you will still have limited protection under what is known as "common law copyright." The whole purpose of copyright is to ensure that only you have the right to use the film as you see fit, and to derive financial gain from your own property. Copyrighting makes it illegal for anyone else to take a print of your film and sell or exhibit it for gain without your knowledge and permission.

If you are working on a documentary intensively involving people and plan to distribute it commercially, it will be advisable to get written releases from people you have photographed. Otherwise, you may be sued for invasion of privacy.

preparing for the mix

If you have two or more 16mm magnetic tracks which make up your sound, the final sound track is assembled in a sound studio in a procedure called "the mix."

The mixing studio is equipped with playback machines called dubbers, which are interlocked so that all the tracks you have created can be played in sync with the picture and each other. In order for this to take place, each track must have a start mark which corresponds with a start mark at the head of the work print. Most 16mm films are now begun with a standardized SMPTE, or numbered, leader. This begins with several feet of film for threading the projector, then contains a frame labeled "Picture Start." After this follows a series of numbers at regular intervals from 8 to 2, representing a countdown in seconds to the first frame of the picture.

The sound tracks must begin with leader which is the same length as the leader on the picture. In standard usage, this is white, single-perf film stock. The leader must bear a punch mark that corresponds to the picture start mark. Signify the punch mark with the word START, and title each track at the very head: e.g., HEAD DIAL A (beginning of Dialogue A), or HEAD FX B (beginning of Sound Effects B), and also write the title of the film. Similarly, at the end of each track, mark the leader TAIL DIAL A, TAIL FX B, etc. In this way, the technicians at the sound lab will be able to line up the tracks in the dubbers with the picture in the projector (see photo 105).

If you have not used SMPTE leader at the beginning of your film, there is a standardized frame count of 4 feet, 32 frames (in 16mm) from the start mark to the first frame of picture or sound, whichever comes first. This distance is not arbitrary, but has to do with the time it takes the dubbers to reach and maintain a constant speed.

It should be noted at this point that mixing studios are not set up for the Super 8 gauge. If, however, you have a Super 8 picture and have cut your sound in 16mm magnetic stock by using one of the Super 8/16mm cutting consoles mentioned in chapter 11, you can, of course, mix your sound against a cue sheet at a mixing studio. The cue sheet is a sound log that indicates which sound is on which track at any given moment or at any given frame of picture.

making a sound log

The most time-consuming part of preparing for the mix is making up the sound log. Think of the log as a musical score which the mixer follows like a conductor in mixing your sound. It tells him which types of sound you have, where they are and when they are coming up (see Fig. 21 in the appendix). It also tells him when sounds are to be faded and dissolved.

Generally, the log is composed of vertical columns with each column representing a track. The length of the columns represent the length of the film. A vertical line drawn within a column tells the mixer that sound exists at that point. Its exact position is given by footage numbers at the beginning and end of the line. The footage count is started at the start mark, which is 0 feet, 0 frames. Fades are indicated by arrow designations at the beginning or end of a line. A dissolve is indicated by a simultaneous fade-out and fade-in of sound on two different tracks.

the mix

At the mix, the mixer sits before a sound console, which contains the controls for the dubbers, or playback machines, facing a screen on which the film is projected during the mix. The picture and the dubbers are interlocked and all will start instantaneously from the start marks indicated on your tracks. At the starting position, a footage counter underneath the screen indicates a zero count. By reading your log against this counter as the film progresses, the mixer knows when the sound is coming up on each of the tracks. Consult the sound lab before the mix, since the footage counters at some labs will read only in 35mm feet. This will mean you will have to convert the 16mm footage numbers on your log to 35mm footage by multiplying the 16mm footage times 2.5.

By working the controls on the console, the mixer can give each sound the right volume and frequency equalization; for instance, if a voice is too "bassy," he can depress the lower frequencies.

Usually it takes a number of rehearsals and trial takes before the mixer has mastered the log. In some studios, the dubbers and picture can remain interlocked and roll back immediately to a point where the mixer has made a mistake. A particularly difficult part where the mixer has many things to do can be repeated for as many times as it takes him to get it right.

Mixing time is very expensive, about one-hundred dollars an hour, and the better your tracks are laid out and the more care that was taken at the time of transfer to keep the sound uniform, the less the mixer will have to do. A half-hour film will require about three or four hours of mixing time.

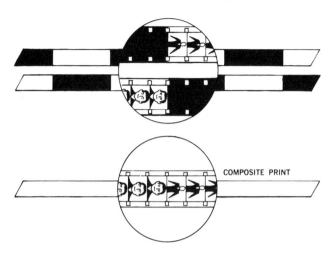

matching the original and cutting the a & b rolls

Once the cut has become final and the mix has taken place, the original is prepared into A & B rolls. This checkerboard method of cutting the original into two rolls of film (shown in the figure below) is designed to eliminate any indication of splices in the final print.

In 35mm there is a small area of black between frames, called the "frame line." It is on this frame line that splices are made, so that they do not cut into the actual frame and are not seen on the screen. In 16mm, the frames are practically touching each other with only the thinnest black line between frames. A normal cement splice would overlap on a portion of the adjoining frame and be seen on the screen.

The shots are alternated between the A and the B roll: the first shot and all other odd-numbered shots are put on the A roll and the second and other even-numbered shots on the B roll. When the second shot goes to the B roll, black leader (dense black film) continues the A roll, and so on. The cement splicing which must overlap onto a frame is done so that the overlap is always made onto the black leader, and in this way never prints through onto the printing stock (see Fig. 19). This is the main purpose of using A & B rolls.

The printing stock goes through the printer twice, once with the A roll and once with the B roll and the optical sound track. If you have done your titles in white lettering on a black background, the title shot is put in place of black leader on either

COMPOSITE PRINT

(*Fig.* 19) The checkerboard of A & B roll technique to eliminate splice lines from the final print

roll and the letters will print through the shot carried by the opposite roll.

In preparing the A & B rolls, you will need a synchronizer and a hot splicer. The hot splicer is a cement splicer (chapter 10) which is heated to make more durable cement bonds. Shots are first "pulled" from the original: the whole shot is cut from the original with scissors, given a number and hung in a film bin. Then one printing roll is made up at a time by matching the shots with the work print in the synchronizer. Practice with the hot splicer until your splices are perfect before you begin to work with the original.

The original is lined up with the work print in the synchronizer by matching the edge numbers. The same edge numbers that were printed through onto the work print will be found on the edge of the original. Remember, when you come to cut a dissolve, the length of the original will be longer than the length of the shot in the work print. This extra length is half the length of the dissolve or overlap, plus two or three extra frames, which are necessary to permit the activation of the shutter in the printer. Consult your lab on this matter before cutting your original.

Dissolves are made by overlapping shots on the A & B rolls. (Fig. 20). The printer aperture is gradually closed on the tail of the first shot. When the opposite roll goes through, it is gradually opened at the beginning of the second shot. In this way, a graduated double exposure is effected. The length of the overlap determines the length of the dissolve.

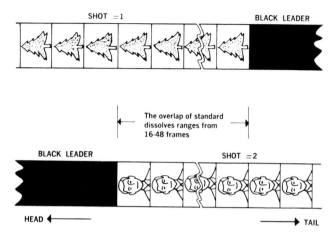

(*Fig.* 20) Dissolves are made by overlapping shots on the A and B rolls.

preparing printing leaders

The leaders of the A & B rolls must have printer's start marks. There should be at least five feet of black leader between the printer's start mark and the first frame of picture, and an equivalent length of leader ahead of the start mark for threading the printing machine. If you use SMPTE leader, there should be a few feet of leader between the head of the SMPTE leader and the printer's start mark.

the optical track

When the sound is mixed, it will be put on a piece of $\frac{1}{4}$-inch tape called the "master." It will then be transferred by the sound lab to a piece of film of the gauge you are working in, called the "optical track." The optical track is blank except for the very edge, which has the sound printed onto it by means of a device called a galvanometer. This device changes the signal from the master tape into a light pattern which is then printed onto the edge of the film outside the picture frame area. In the final printing, the optical track is exposed with the original to make up a "composite print" of your film to include both sound and picture (see photo 105).

In order for the optical track to ultimately be lined up with the original in the printer, it, too, must have a start mark. This is something which is prepared before the mix in the following way: using the synchronizer, find the frame on the leader of the dialogue track which corresponds to the number two on the SMPTE leader, or the frame which is 3 feet, 24 frames from the start mark. Mark this frame. Take a frame-length of magnetic tape with adhesive backing, called "bleep tape," and place it lengthwise on the nonsprocketed edge of the track on the frame you have marked.

The bleep tape is placed on the edge because, although 16mm magnetic stock is completely coated with oxide, the transferred sound is recorded and read on the outer edge only. The bleep tape is recorded with an audible signal. At the mix, when the picture leader passes the number two, a "beep" will be heard played back by the dialogue dubber. This short signal is later recorded onto the optical track and, after the track has been processed, can be seen near the head of the optical track as a dense oscillation one frame long. This is the only mark you will have to line up the optical track with the original.

When you line up the optical track, first find the frame which corresponds to the printer's start marks on the A & B rolls. Then advance the track 26 frames and mark the printer's start mark. The sound must be advanced by this amount for printing, since projectors, by design, read the sound 26 frames in advance of the picture.

(*Photo* 106) (from left to right) 1—The work print at the juncture of two shots. 2—The A roll of camera original showing one shot spliced to black leader. 3—The B roll showing black leader spliced to the other shot. 4—The optical sound track. 5—The composite release print of both shots and sound track.

a & b rolls and release printing

When the A & B rolls go through the printer, not only must the printing shutters be timed for the dissolves and fades, but each shot must be timed separately with regard to exposure and color. This is the job of the "timer" at the lab. The first attempt at getting the correct density, or exposure, and color balance for each shot is called the first "answer print."

You will then go over this print shot by shot with the timer and make necessary corrections. The corrected answer print is called the second answer print. Depending on the evenness of the original color balance and exposure, as well as any special effects you may desire, such as with day-for-night shots, you may well go through three, four or more answer prints before you get a print with which you are satisfied.

Final prints made after a satisfactory answer print has been obtained are called "release prints." These are the prints that will be available for exhibition and sale. If many prints are to be made, the A & B rolls are printed onto an internegative from which the release prints will be made. There is some deterioration of color and contrast, but it is much cheaper to print from one piece of film than from two.

summary

To complete your film after editing, mark your work print for fades, dissolves, titles and any other special effects. Order or shoot titles, either to superimpose or to appear by themselves, and cut a duplicate into the work print. Prepare all the sound tracks for the mix by aligning and marking all leaders to correspond to the picture leader. Prepare the sound log for the mixer, then have the sound studio mix your film. Ask them to make an optical transfer of the sound track for final composite printing. Finally, cut the original picture into A & B rolls to match the work print. Take the A & B picture rolls, along with the sound track, to the lab and ask for a composite print. Work with the lab timer on the first answer print, shot by shot, until he has corrected the whole film for density (lightness and darkness) and color balance. Continue with subsequent prints until you have the quality you want.

13. SHOWING THE FILM

Judging the sound and image quality of your final print will depend to a large degree on the condition of projector and the screening room. Since the screening of the first answer print, like the screening of the rushes, is an emotionally trying experience for the filmmaker, you should know something about the elements that affect the outcome.

The dominant element affecting the image quality is the projection lens. Its quality varies greatly, depending upon the make of the projector and the condition of the lens, and whether the gauge is Super 8 or 16mm. The differences are more noticeable in 16mm, where the requirements of craftsmanship have been more demanding. You will probably find yourself using a Bell & Howell Filmosound projector, which is the standard projection system in most schools and screening rooms. This projector costs around $750. Although this is a good-quality, dependable projector, to see what you can be missing, try to project your film on a projector of the quality of a Siemens or Sonorex, which run from $3,000 to $4,000.

The work of the best 16mm shooting lenses will look soft when projected by an inexpensive projector, but a fingerprint smudge on the front element of the best projection lens will have the same effect. Check the front element and remove any smudges in the same manner as you would with a camera lens. Of course, there is always the question of focus. Any projection lens must be focused correctly on the screen.

Image brightness is affected by the quality of the screen, the brightness of the projector lamp and the distance, or throw, between the projector and the screen. If a long throw is required of the projector, the image may look dull or dark on the best screen. The material the screen is made of should be highly reflective. Beaded glass and silvered surfaces are the most common. You can project a sharp image onto a piece of white cardboard or a white plasterboard wall, but you cannot expect the image to be as bright.

The screening room should be capable of being totally blacked out. Any additional light to the light from the projector will cause the image to look dull. If the room cannot be entirely blacked out, then a special "black" screen, designed for projection in rooms with a certain amount of ambient light, should be used.

Lastly, a projection bulb near the end of its life will make the image look dull and reddish. The color balance of your film can also be affected by the design of the projection bulb. Certain high-intensity projection bulbs designed for long throws will cause a shift of the color spectrum toward the blue end, giving your whole film a bluish look. For the showing of a color film in a large hall or amphitheater with this kind of bulb, a special color-

(*Photo* 107) The Sonorex double-system projector. This projector can project a composite print, or work print in sync with a separate magnetic sound track.

corrected print of the film must be made.

Make sure that the projector on which you screen your film is in good condition and that the gate is clean; otherwise, your print may be badly scratched throughout its entire length. If the scratch occurs in the area of the gate below the projection aperture, you will not see the scratch until the next time you project it. If you are not sure whether a projector will scratch, run a piece of test film through a couple of times.

Prints inevitably get scratched with use and you will not always have control over projection. Scratches on the base side of the film look black on the screen, and can be treated by a scratch-removal service. The scratch appears black because it defracts the projection beam. Scratch removal fills in or buffs out the scratches.

The reproduction of your sound track can be adversely affected by a number of things. The worst offender is the adjustment of the small lamp inside the projector which reads the optical track in the area of the sound drum (a revolving drum below and in front of the projection gate). If it is not beamed through the center of the optical sound at the edge of the film, the high end of the frequency range may be greatly depressed. Some projectors are designed so that you can adjust this light yourself.

The second worst offender is the placement of the speaker. Most portable projectors have a small speaker in the body of the projector. Not only does this yield a limited reproduction of the base frequencies, but the sound coming from behind the audience has an unnatural relationship with the image. Try to use a larger extension speaker placed beneath the screen whenever possible.

Even with good speaker placement, the sound can be ruined by the acoustics of the room. A large empty room constructed with hard, reflecting materials may make the sound reverberate so badly that dialogue becomes unintelligible. Curtains, carpets, upholstered chairs and, above all, a large audience will improve the situation.

As has been said before, for real involvement in a film, we, the audience, don't want to be reminded of the mechanics of the medium. One such distraction is the sound of the projector. If a projection booth is available, the projector is beamed through a glass window which seals off any annoying mechanical sound from the audience; otherwise, place the projector well back from the audience.

View your film away from the projector and in the center of the room. From the side, image shape is somewhat distorted and brightness is lost. If you are too close to the screen, the image will appear less sharp and skipping effects will be pronounced. The farther back you are, the smaller the image will appear and the closer you will be to projection noise.

film festivals and cooperatives

Once you have made a film that you are proud of, you will want to expose it to a larger audience than just your friends or your class, as they will seldom give you an unbiased reaction. There is an ever-increasing number of film festivals that will accept amateur and student work. *Variety*, the New York show-business weekly, publishes a film-festival directory which covers worldwide exhibition and competition. CINE and Kodak both sponsor amateur festivals.

Some other well-known festivals in the United States where films may be seen and prizes awarded include the Chicago, Atlanta, San Francisco and

Columbus film festivals, as well as the Midwest Film Festival at Evanston, Illinois; the American Film Festival in New York; and the New York Film Festival at Lincoln Center.

If you think your film deserves a wider audience, you may want to place a copy of your film on deposit with a film cooperative, such as the Film-Makers Cooperative in New York and the Canyon Cinema Cooperative in California. Your film would be entered in their catalogues, and you collect 75 percent of the rental fee, which is set by you. They do not actively sell your film other than placing it in their catalogues.

distribution

As your films become more professional, you will want to know about film distribution. This is the aspect of film that has to do with how films are sold and rented, what income may be expected and what kinds of audiences will see your films.

We will say little about theatrical distribution because it is enormously specialized and extremely difficult to break into. If the fiction film is your métier, Godspeed. Distribution is mostly controlled by a very few, very large, well-known name companies, though there are a number of smaller independent distributors. In the feature market, the first step after the script is written is to get a distribution guarantee.

Television is an omnivorous market for film, but almost all television films are contracted for before they are made, and the contracts, in most cases, are made with professional producers. At current film-production costs, no one is willing to trust the making of even a single film to a beginner.

Television can be a potential source of income, but don't bank on it. If you have already made a film and it is good enough for national distribution, it is possible—just barely—that you may get someone in either network or local television to screen it, and they, in turn, may recommend it. Educational television, in particular, is receptive to the work of unknown filmmakers.

The best place for your film, especially if it is short, may be professional 16mm distribution. There is a huge educational-film marketplace that most people (including many filmmakers) know nothing about. Large distributing companies, like McGraw-Hill, Encyclopedia Brittanica Films and Coronet, each have thousands of titles in their catalogues, and they sell and rent prints to schools, libraries, churches and clubs in large numbers each year. There are also many smaller organizations, like Churchill, International Film Foundation, ACI and Film Images, with fewer but superior films. You may approach any of these companies, show them your film and ask them to distribute it for you. If your film is fiction or experimental, try Audio-Brandon, Pyramid, Grove Press and Film Images. They will accept your film if they like it, and lay out whatever sum of money is required to promote it. You will receive a royalty on every print they sell. If sales are good, the royalties can be substantial; but remember, most films never earn back their production cost.

professional organizations
and periodicals

There are many national organizations and periodi-
cals that can help you learn about filmmaking and
about marketing your films. EFLA, the Educational
Film Library Association (17 West 60th Street, New
York, N.Y. 10023), publishes a magazine called
Sightlines and, in addition to sponsoring the an-
nual American Film Festival, is a primary source of
information on educational films. The American
Film Institute, with offices in Washington (1815 H
Street NW, Washington, D.C. 20006) and Beverly
Hills (501 Doheny Road, Beverly Hills, Calif. 90210),
concerns itself with the feature film, film preserva-
tion and screen education, and awards annual
fellowships and grants for short film projects. The
Center for Understanding Media, in New York (267
West 25th Street, New York, N.Y. 10001) specializes
in film education in schools. CINE, housed in the
National Education Association (NEA) building in
Washington (1201 16th Street NW, Washington,
D.C. 20036), not only conducts semiannual film
festivals for both amateurs and professionals, but
enters winning films in foreign film festivals. The
AECT (Association for Educational Communications and Technology, 1201 16th Street NW, Washington, D.C. 20036), a division of the NEA, is the
national service organization for teachers using
film, filmstrips and tapes in the classroom. The
AECT holds an annual convention each spring with
an ambitious program of meetings and workshops
designed to provide information on the above media, from the simplest to the most complex level.

The American Library Association (50 East Huron Street, Chicago, Ill. 60611) has information about the use of film in libraries.

On a local level, most states have audiovisual associations which keep their membership abreast of current events in the field through regular publications and statewide or regional convocations. In New York City, the New York Film Council conducts monthly programs which are open to all members of the local film community. The Museum of Modern Art (11 West 53rd Street, New York, N.Y. 10019) and the Whitney Museum (Madison Avenue at 75th Street, New York, N.Y. 10021) regularly schedule film programs. The Donnell Library, across the street from the Museum of Modern Art, houses a collection of films as well as books and periodicals on film.

Some periodicals on film include: *The Journal of the University Film Association* (Department of Photography and Film, The Ohio State University, Columbus, Ohio 43210), for film criticism and scholarship; *The American Cinematographer* (1782 North Orange Drive, Hollywood, Calif. 90028), equipment and technique; *Business Screen* (Harcourt Brace Jovanovich, Inc., 757 Third Avenue, New York, N.Y. 10017), industrial films; *Previews* (R. R. Bowker, 1180 Avenue of the Americas, New York, N.Y. 10036), listings and reviews; *Film Library Quarterly* (Film Library Information Council, P.O. Box 348, Radio City Station, New York, N.Y. 10019), criticism, articles and reviews; *Media & Methods* (North American Publishing, 134 North 13th Street, Philadelphia, Pa. 19107), media education; *Film Comment* (1865 Broadway, New York, N.Y. 10023), criticism; *Filmmakers Newsletter* (Suncraft International, P.O. Box 482, Marblehead, Mass. 01945), independent film activity; *Film News* (250 West 57th Street, New York, N.Y. 10019), educational film; *Film Critic* (American Federation of Film Societies,

333 Avenue of the Americas, New York, N.Y. 10014), film-society news and criticism; *Film Culture* (175 Lexington Avenue, New York, N.Y. 10003), criticism; and *Super-8 Filmmaker* (145 East 49th Street, New York, N.Y. 10017), Super 8 news.

in conclusion

If you continue with filmmaking, you will spend much of your time perfecting technique. The more refined technique becomes, the more problems there will be to solve. In an important sense, there is never more excitement to filmmaking than in your first experience. You can proceed with the least amount of worry and go directly about getting the center of your idea or experience onto film.

Earning a living as a filmmaker is difficult but possible. You will have to work vigorously for your first job, overcome many obstacles in fighting for a small place in an overcrowded field and be willing, at least initially, to earn less money than many people doing less demanding work. If you are not easily discouraged, then go ahead.

Knowledge and practice in filmmaking will give you a much greater appreciation of the film medium. It will also give you a new way of looking at individuals and their problems in communication. Filmmakers find their work enjoyable, challenging and filled with opportunities to travel and gain insight into other cultures.

If you take up film, either as a hobby or as a profession, you will undoubtedly derive great satisfaction from your work. The authors of this book hope you will find as much pleasure in film as they have.

APPENDIX

Preparing Material for the Sound Mix*

Following are the specifications set up by a leading sound studio for submitting material to them for a mix. While these requirements vary slightly from studio to studio, they can serve as general guidelines.

1. All rolls should be clearly identified at both head and tail.

2. All rolls should be filled out to the same length. There should be 15 additional feet of leader before the start mark and 30 feet of additional leader after the last sound.

3. There should be only one start mark on each roll. The start mark is at 0 feet, 0 frames. At 3 feet, 24 frames, a B (for "beep") is marked on both picture and tracks, and a beep applied to a

synchronous track. Use only paste-on beeps—if you do not have any, we will apply one. At 4 feet, 32 frames, the first frame of picture and track occurs.

4. Use only *white* splicing tape for splicing sound tracks. Clear picture tape should not be used for splicing tracks.

5. Leader in sound tracks has to be used with its shiny *base* on the same side of the film as the dull magnetic oxide. Otherwise the soft leader emulsion scrapes off onto the playback heads of the dubbers and causes the sound to be muffled.

6. Cue sheets should be prepared. Put the start mark at 0 feet, 0 frames, on the synchronizer. For a 16mm film the footages should be expressed as 16mm feet and tenths—four frames equals a tenth of a foot. Thus 24 feet, 32 frames, would be entered as 24.8. It is not necessary to convert 16mm footages to 35mm footages.

7. No reel of 16mm film can be longer than 1100 feet.

8. If additional sources of sound are to be used at the mix, they should be discussed with us in advance. Such sources might be: live narration, phonograph records, cassette tapes, music or effects from our library, or effects loops from our library. If you have prepared loops from 16mm magnetic, they should be supplied to us ahead of time so that we may copy them to a specially durable ¼-inch tape.

9. If there is single perf in the picture, the head leader should also be single perf.

10. Material may be submitted on either reels or cores, heads or tails out, whichever is most convenient for you.

Some hints that we suggest you follow to save mixing time, raise quality, and reduce the chance of mistakes:

1. Prepare your picture so that it will run through the projector.

The best thing to bring to the mix is a "scratch" or "slop" print, a reversal print made from the edited work print. If last-minute changes are then made in the work print, make sure that the slop print has been conformed to it.

Next best is a work print spliced on both sides with perforated tape. One-sided splices are not recommended. If they must be used, their chances of running properly are better if they are made on that side of the work print that is toward the projector lamp (the emulsion side of work prints made from a camera original).

It is sometimes not good enough simply to complete the other side of one-sided splices just before a mix or interlock. If the ends of the film have pulled apart slightly, leaving a space, it will not run through a projector, even though it has been running satisfactorily through rotating prism editing machines or viewers. Splices with such gaps in them must be taken apart and completely remade.

Guillotine-type splicers are a frequent source of trouble when they do not completely punch out the perforations. It is sometimes necessary to re-punch the perforations or use a razor blade to clean up the flaps and hinges of splicing tape.

2. The tracks should be in good condition.

They should be spliced with *white* tape. (We use 3M brand.) Clear picture tape or substandard white tape is not suitable, partly because its adhesive tends to ooze out onto the track. Another problem is that splices made with it will run on editing machines, but studio dubbers, which have greater tension for high-quality playback, are certain to pull the ends of the splice apart. Because it is not easy to use two kinds of tape with guillotine splicers, they are again the most frequent cause of trouble. If for your convenience you have used clear tape while editing, remake the splices with white tape before you mix or interlock.

Don't use grease pencils or china markers on the tracks. Use a flow pen or Magic Marker instead. Grease or wax anywhere on the tracks or leader—even on the base side—eventually finds its way to the playback heads and causes a "wow" or dropouts. In those cases where you *must* use a grease pencil—tapping music tracks to find the beat, for example—clean it off carefully afterwards. (Most film cleaners dissolve magnetic oxide, so just scrub with a soft cloth.)

If at all possible, do not use double-perf fill leader in 16mm sound tracks. Mechanical agitation of the dubber heads by the sprocket holes may cause unwanted noises in playback. More importantly, double perf gives you the chance of making an error with horrid consequences during a hasty revision of the tracks. Needless to say, *never* use double perf for the head or tail leader of sound tracks. Try to avoid using pieces of leader that have many splices. The head leader should be splice-free.

If you have a diagonal splicer, use it for the sound tracks. The louder the background noise of your dialogue tracks, the more chance you have of causing clicks by using a straight splicer. Diagonal splicers minimize the chance of clicks or pops at the splice. They run more evenly through the machines, causing less wow and flutter and fewer dropouts, a particularly important advantage in music editing.

When there is unmodulated magnetic at the head of a piece of music, leave it there to minimize wow at the music entrance. If there is not, you may add three or four feet of virgin magnetic.

Leave as much room tone or presence in your voice tracks as possible. Don't cut things so short that you clip off breaths or the ends of words. You should, however, remove anything that you will clearly not want in your final mix—slates, beeps, recorder starts and stops, instructions to the cameraman, cries of "Cut! That's great!" and so forth. Listen carefully for these small unwanted sounds when you have your tracks on a synchronizer sound head. They frequently pass unnoticed when they are masked by editing machine noise.

3. How many tracks should you have and how should they be laid out?

Do not simply label three rolls A, B and C and insert the elements of the film in them wherever there happens to be space. Try instead to follow a pattern that is logical and will be easily understood. Divide the sounds into categories. The usual categories, reading from left to right on the cue sheet, are: DIALOGUE NARRATION (or VOICE-OVER) MUSIC EFFECTS.

If your film contains these four kinds of sounds, you had better begin by thinking that you need four tracks. The sounds need to be separated in this way to do two things: first, to make it easy to locate the track on which a sound is expected; and second, to feed that sound automatically into the specialized mixing channel best equipped to deal with it.

When do you need additional tracks within the four major categories? Obviously, if one piece of music is going to dissolve into another, you will need to make MUSIC A and MUSIC B. If two effects occur simultaneously or dissolve into one another, they appear to require EFFECTS A and EFFECTS B.

Does this mean that you cannot put a few effects on the music track, or that voice-over cannot be put into unused space in the dialogue track? Will you always have to make eight tracks when it seems that five would do? Of course not. If the mixer has sufficient time between sounds belonging to different categories, he can handle deviations from a rigorous pattern, as long as the following general principles are observed:

Deviations from the usual content of a given track should be clearly labeled.

The voice tracks should not have music or effects on them.

If one piece of sound fades out and another immediately cuts in at full volume, or a cutout is followed by a fade-in, the two pieces should be on separate tracks.

If two sounds follow each other closely, are *alike* in volume or quality, and are to be made *different,* they should be on separate tracks.

If two sounds are *different,* and are to be made *alike,* they should also be on separate tracks. It is for this reason that dialogue is sometimes split into A and B tracks. Splitting the dialogue tracks might also give you the chance to correct severe background noise mismatches. Save the little trims when you cut the dialogue and overlap the background noise when you split the track. The mixer may be able to make short dissolves to mask the abruptness of the cuts.

There are clear artistic and economic advantages to mixing a film from several tracks, but it is also clearly inconvenient to handle several tracks at once during all the stages of editing your film. Therefore, there are two things you should do: First, put off as much sound editing as possible until the picture has been frozen in its final form. The dialogue and picture must be cut simultaneously, of course, and it is a powerful artistic device to cut picture to music; but it is usually easier to cut sound to picture than the other way around. Second, for convenience in editing, put tracks together that you know must eventually be separated. Interlock the film in that form, doing the routine mechanical task of splitting the tracks only when you know you are ready to mix.

4. The interlock

No procedure is more valuable in achieving artistic and technical excellence—and economy—than interlocking your film at the sound studio before you mix it. We encourage interlocks by charging a great deal less for interlock time than for mixing time.

Schedule the interlock far enough ahead of time—two days, for a one-reel film—so that you will be able to make the corrections and changes that you require. If you are in doubt as to how the tracks should be split, the interlock is an excellent time to discuss it with the mixer. He can also make loops or transfers of room tone to fill holes in your tracks. If there are any doubts about sync, it is far better to resolve them at the interlock than at the mix.

A cue sheet should be prepared for the interlock. Even a simple cue sheet will help the mixer and give you both a place to make notes about possible revisions.

5. The cue sheets

The mixer wants the cue sheet to tell him what is on the tracks as he receives them, not what is supposed to result from the mix.

If you call us ahead of time, we will supply you with our special cue sheets; but every sound studio uses a similar form, and you can make cue sheets on blank paper if you like.

The sheet is divided into vertical columns, one for each track. The order in which the tracks are logged from left to right is important. Most mixers will want them in the same order, which should be: dialogue, narration, music, effects.

In each column, vertical lines are drawn whenever a piece of sound is playing, with its beginning and end labeled in that column with their corresponding footages. Room tone or background noise in the voice tracks should also be indicated. The cue sheet is analogous to what you would see if the tracks were rolled out side by side on an airport runway, but the lines need not be drawn to any particular or consistent scale, so long as the relationships are correctly shown—lines overlap when the tracks do, and don't when they don't.

Brief labels on complex tracks are a help—"child's steps" and "hooves" if the two are playing together, for example; fade-ins and fade-outs can be indicated with drawn V's, but you should not waste time on either complicated or obvious instructions to the mixer. If you are going to be at the mix, he wants you as his esthetic guide, the cue sheet as a road map.

6. Synchronization

Small errors in synchronization can haunt you

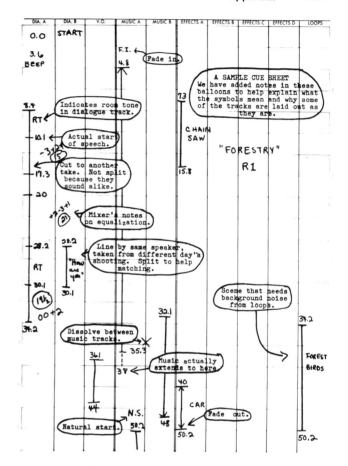

(*Fig.* 21) A cue sheet

through several answer prints, and serious errors can ruin a production as surely as camera failure.

The dailies should be transferred and synced while you are shooting, rather than saving them until the end of production. If that is not possible, at least submit the ¼-inch tapes to the sound studio for audition, so that any failure of sync signal can be reported as soon as it occurs. Even if the tape sync signal appears to be adequate, the transfers may not match the picture for a large number of reasons, so true safety is achieved only by syncing as you shoot.

If material will not remain in sync throughout a take, do not immediately begin adding or subtracting frames here and there to correct it. Instead, bring the picture, track and original ¼-inch tapes to us, and we will advise you on what procedure to follow for diagnosis and correction.

Once the dailies have been synced up, check them by screening if at all possible. They will eventually be judged in projection, not by the somewhat deceptive image on an editing machine. Seeing your dialogue on a big screen for the first time at the mix is always a surprise. Seeing it out of sync is always an expensive shock.

After the dailies have been checked, have them edge-coded. The small additional cost is more than made up for by the artistic freedom and freedom from worry that only edge-coding can give you.

GLOSSARY

A & B rolls—The two rolls of original film which, by alternating shots with black leader, are used to make the final print so that splices do not show. (See checkerboard cutting, photo 105, Fig. 19.)

Angle of acceptance—The field of vision, or area, that a lens "sees." The angle of acceptance of a wide-angle lens is greater than the angle of acceptance of a telephoto lens

Animation—Creating the illusion of motion by the technique of filming still material, such as drawings, frame by frame, and introducing gradual changes between each frame

Aperture—The opening in either the lens or camera through which the light is admitted to the film

ASA rating—The U.S. standard system of rating film emulsion speed

Assembly—The first attempt in a film to link all the shots in sequential order following the plan for the finished film

Axis of action—An imaginary line drawn through the center of action. A sequence of shots must all be taken from one side of this line so as not to disorient the viewer.

Back light—A light used behind a subject to create a halo effect

Barney—A soft covering, such as a blanket, used to quiet camera noise

Base—The cellulose-acetate carrier upon which the light-sensitive emulsion is coated. The base side of film is shiny, the emulsion side is dull

Bayonet mount—A method of attaching a lens to the camera. The bayonet or "Arri" mounted lens is simply pressed into place and locked with a slight twist. (See C-mount.)

Black leader—Cellulose-acetate film coated with o-paque black emulsion; used primarily to separate shots on original A & B rolls

Blimp—A rigid, sound-absorbing camera cover to reduce camera noise for sound shooting

Blocking—Placing the actors and planning their movements within a set

Boominess—That quality of a recording which accentuates the bass, or lower frequencies, so that spoken words, for example, become "muddy" and less distinct

C-mount—One of the two common methods of attaching a lens to the camera. The C-mount lens is screwed into the lens socket. (See bayonet mount.)

Cardioid—A microphone pattern shaped like a heart, with sensitivity greatest toward the front and least toward the back

Cell animation—The animation technique where the subject matter is drawn on layers of acetate. In this way the foreground can change while the background remains constant

Cement splice—The joining of two pieces of film by scraping the emulsion off part of one frame of the first piece, applying film cement and overlapping the second piece onto the scraped portion of the first. This method is always used in making up A & B rolls. (See Mylar splice.)

Checkerboard cutting—Making original A & B rolls by alternating each shot with black leader. Since the A roll will have shots where the B roll has black leader, and vice versa, the effect is that of a checkerboard. (See photo 105, Fig. 19.)

Cinéma vérité—A film made without script or formal direction; a visual record of real action

Clapstick—A slating board with hinged top producing an audible and visual signal which enables the sound and picture relationship to be established in sync. (See photo 74.)

Close-up—A close shot of the subject, most commonly a head-and-shoulders shot of an actor

Coding—A method of relating the work print to the original or to the magnetic sound track by printing a series of corresponding numbers along the edges

Color balance—The visible spectrum ranges from red to violet. Color balance is the emphasis a source of light gives to one section of this spectrum: shooting a sunset would be heavily balanced toward red; shooting a scene in deep shade would be balanced toward blue

Color temperature—A measurement, in degrees Kelvin, of the color balance of a light source

Composite print—The picture and the (optical) sound track combined on one print

Continuity—The quality of unbroken narrative action in a series of shots

Contrast—The relationship of light to dark in the film image. A "contrasty" image accentuates both dark and light and has few middle tones

Conversion filter—A filter (Wratten no. 85) used when shooting exteriors with film balanced for artificial light

Copyright—The right given to authors to control the duplication and exhibition of their work for a period of twenty-eight years. This may be renewed for an additional twenty-eight years

Core—A small plastic center upon which film or magnetic stock may be wound without the use of a reel

Critical focus—The point of focus at which the image is sharpest

Cutaway—A shot related to the narrative, but not directly to the principal subject, such as an audience reaction to a speaker

Day-for-night photography—The technique of shooting during the day so that the finished film will look like it was shot at night. This is accomplished by underexposing, not showing sky and using side light

Daylight film—Color film balanced for exterior light

Daylight loading spool—100- or 200-foot rolls of film mounted on spools which allow for daylight loading of camera. 400- and 1200-foot rolls of film are mounted on cores and must be loaded and unloaded in a changing bag or darkroom

Decibel—A measurement of sound intensity. One decibel (db) is the smallest variation in volume that can be detected by the human ear

Depth of field—The range between the closest and most distant points to the camera throughout which continuous sharp focus is found

Dissolve—Simultaneous fading-out of one shot as another fades in so that there is an overlap of images

Dolly shot—Shot taken from a moving platform

Double-perf film—Film which has sprocket perforations at both edges

Double-system sound—A method of filming where picture and sound are recorded simultaneously, with sound recorded on a separate tape recorder. (See single-system sound.)

Dubber—Sound-reproducing machine used in a sound-mixing studio to play back sprocketed magnetic tracks in sync with picture

Edge numbers—Numbers printed at the edge of raw stock which are developed when the film is processed. These numbers are usually printed through onto the work print for convenient matching of the two

Emulsion—A light-sensitive chemical coated onto the film base

Exposure—The amount of light falling on the film. Exposure is set by adjusting the aperture of the lens according to the amount of light falling on the subject

Exposure meter—A light-measuring device. (See photo 41.)

Fade-in—A gradual change at the beginning of a shot going from black to full image brightness

Fade-out—Reverse of fade-in; the image gradually goes to black at the end of a shot

Fast motion—The technique of speeding up action by shooting film at a rate slower than the rate of projection

Fill—Film used as spacer between the sound elements in a magnetic track

Fill light—A secondary light used to fill in the heavy shadows created by the key, or main, light

Film gauge—The width of standard film stock in millimeters: Super 8mm, 16mm, 35mm

Film plane—The area in the camera gate through which the film moves as it is being exposed

Film speed—The sensitivity of film emulsion to light

Film viewer—An editing tool used in conjunction with two rewinds for viewing the film. (See photo 83.)

Filter—A thin piece of glass or gelatin mounted either just in front or behind the lens to alter the quality of the light. The three main filters are conversion, neutral density and polarizing

Filter slot—A slot in the camera behind the lens into which a filter may be inserted

Fine cut—The stage of editing just before the final cut when the work print approximates the finished film

First answer print—The first composite print made by a laboratory from the A & B rolls and the optical sound track

Flash frames—The two or three frames at the beginning and end of each shot, and the frame between two shots, which are overexposed due to the start-up and slowdown of the camera motor

Frame—That portion of the film exposed by each opening of the camera shutter. Frame may also refer to the shot as seen by the cameraman through the viewfinder

Freeze frame—An optical effect which stops motion by making multiple exposures of a single frame

Frequency equalization—Decreasing or emphasizing low, middle or high frequencies of a sound track to correct distortion or improve tonal balance

Follow focus—Changing lens focus while shooting to keep a moving subject in sharp focus

Focal length—A distance related to the distance between the optical element of lens and film plane. Telephoto lenses have long focal lengths and wide-angle lenses have short focal lengths

Focus—To adjust the lens so that the image appears sharp

Footage—A measurement of film stock in feet. Commonly used to refer to film that has been shot, such as, "Did you get good footage of the parade?"

f/stop—The numbers (*f*/2, *f*/2.8, *f*/4, *f*/5.6) referring to the various iris openings on a lens which vary the amount of light reaching the film

Gate—That part of the camera (or projector) through which the film passes behind the lens in order to be exposed (or projected)

Grain—The tiny, individual particles that make up film emulsion. A film is "grainy" if we readily see the particles "swimming" on the screen

High-angle shot—A shot angled down from above eye, or normal, level

Hot splicer—A cement splicer with a heated base plate which decreases drying time, used for splicing original in A & B rolls

Incident light—That light falling onto a subject as opposed to the light being reflected by the subject

Intermittent motion—The noncontinuous movement of the film through the camera gate caused by the motion of the pull-down claw

Internegative—An intermediate print made from A & B rolls, permitting multiple release prints to be made from a single picture roll

Iris—A set of intermeshing metal leaves whose purpose is to increase or decrease the lens aperture. (See Fig. 9.)

Jump cut—A cut from one shot to another during a narrative sequence that doesn't flow naturally and disorients the viewer

Kelvin degrees—The unit used to measure color temperature. Sunlight is rated at 7000° K., a 100-watt household bulb at 2850° K

Key light—The main light on a subject

Lap dissolve—(See dissolve.)

Latitude—The range of light, from bright to dark, that a film emulsion will accept

Lavalier—A small microphone worn on the chest

Leader—Several feet of blank film at the head and tail of a print used for threading, and to protect the print from wear

Lens—A series of optical glass elements which collect and focus the image on the film plane in the camera

Lens aperture—(See aperture.)

Light meter—(See exposure meter.)

Lighting ratio—The ratio of the key light plus the fill light to the fill light alone

Long shot—Usually an establishing shot, frequently scenic, showing the subject at a distance

Low-angle shot—A shot angled up from below eye, or normal, level

Magazine—A detachable unit for holding 400- and 1200-foot loads of film on cores. They must be loaded and unloaded either in a darkroom or changing bag

Magnetic stock—The 16mm or 35mm perforated stock with iron-oxide coating, used in editing and mixing sound

Magnetic stripe—A coat of magnetic striping, which can accept a sound track, printed along one edge of the film. In Super 8 and 16mm, the stripe will be on single-perf film, opposite the perforations

Match cutting—Cutting action for continuous flow of movement: i.e., if shot no. 1 shows the subject beginning to rise from his chair, shot no. 2 will begin on the rise just at the point where shot no. 1 left off

Matching—Cutting the original into A & B rolls to match the work print

Medium grey—A middle tone, halfway between black and white, representing the brightness of the average reflecting surface. A reflected light meter should read a medium grey tone, rather than either a very dark or very light part of the subject, to produce accurate exposure

Medium shot—A shot in which the subject is seen at a middle distance, neither in long shot or close-up

Mismatch—Any combination of shots breaking continuity and disorienting the viewer. Example: taking one shot of a subject with sunlight and the next under cloud cover, and cutting these two shots together in a narrative sequence

Mix—The process of putting together all the individual magnetic sound tracks that will make the final sound

Modulation—Controlling a sound recording by increasing or decreasing input volume

Montage—A rapid flow of images with one or more themes

Moviola—The basic editing machine for cutting sound and picture together. Sound and picture can be run together in sync at sound speed, backward or forward, or run independently of each other. A variable speed control on the picture side allows frame-by-frame picture examination

Mylar splice—The standard editing splice made by using adhesive Mylar tape to join two pieces of film together without overlapping frames. (See cement splice.)

Negative—Film that produces images reversed from positive; i.e., black appears as clear, and white as black

Neutral density filter—A filter made of optical glass or gelatin that reduces the amount of light passing through the aperture without altering color or quality.

It is used when high-speed film must be shot in bright sunlight, or when the depth of focus is to be diminished (use of shallow focus) by using a lower f/stop

One-light work print—Making a work print from the original without adjusting the printer light for optimal quality for each shot. It is much less expensive than a "timed" work print, and commonly used for editing purposes

Optical printing—Special effects such as freeze frames and titles, that are processed by an optical printer

Optical track—The sound track printed on separate film stock, as distinguished from the magnetic sound tracks used in editing. The optical track is used in making the final composite print

Out takes—Scenes of original footage not used in the final film

Overexposure—Allowing more light to reach the film than would produce an image of medium brightness. Overexposure produces a "washed-out" image

Pan—Moving the camera from side to side on its vertical axis while shooting, usually from a tripod

Parallax error—The disparity between what the lens sees and what the non-reflex viewfinder sees, due to the minor separation between them

Parallel action—Action occurring in different places at the same time

Polarizing filter—A filter which cuts down glare and reflections on water, metal, glass and sky. It is particularly useful for producing a deep-blue sky and distant detail

Positive—Opposite of negative; i.e., black shows black and white is clear

Presence—The natural sound of any location, called "room tone" indoors

Print—A copy made from film original

Processing—The chemical action on the film in the laboratory which develops the latent image

Prop—A contraction of the word "property"; any object handled by an actor or used to dress a set. If it is real, it is called a practical, or working, prop

Proposal—A simple statement describing an idea for a film

Pull-down claw—The key to the intermittent motion in both camera and projector. A piece of metal which engages the sprocket hole, pulls the film down one frame, then withdraws and prepares to repeat while the frame just pulled into place is exposed

Quartz light—A relatively new kind of photographic light that is much more efficient than the older tungsten lights

Raw stock—Unexposed film to be used in the camera

Reaction shot—A shot showing some response to the main action

Reflected light—Light reflected by the subject toward the camera. (See incident light.)

Reflex viewfinder—A camera viewfinder that shows the shot to the cameraman precisely as the film "sees" it, since the image is formed by the camera lens

Registration pin—A small metal pin which holds the film rock-steady in the gate during exposure; found only in the best professional cameras

Release—The permission to photograph persons or property obtained as protection against a suit for invasion of privacy

Release prints—Prints mass-produced for distribution

Reversal film—Film which, when used as original, produces a positive rather than a negative image when processed

Reverse angle—A camera angle, varying approximately 180° from the preceding shot; often a point-of-view shot

Rewinds—The pair of geared cranks and spindles used to wind film; usually mounted on an editing bench

Room tone—See presence.

Rough cut—The first attempt to give the film some shape; made after the assembly, but before the fine cut

Rushes—The work-print footage made from the original of a day's shooting

SMPTE leader—Standard numbered leader specified by the Society of Motion Picture and Television Engineers. The purpose of the SMPTE leader is to allow the projector to reach full speed, and to allow the projectionist to focus

Scene contrast—The range between the darkest and lightest elements in a particular scene

Script—The final written blueprint for a film, including scene description and dialogue

Sequence—A series of shots related in time and space in a narrative manner

Shooting script—A script with detailed notations on sets and props, blocking and camera direction

Shooting ratio—The film footage actually shot compared to the footage used in the final film

Shot—The continuous length of one take from camera start to camera stop

Shotgun microphone—An ultradirectional microphone with greatest sensitivity in a very narrow cone pattern to its front

Shutter—A rotating disc which prevents exposure of the film during its pull-down, and permits its exposure when stationary

Sibilance—The high-energy, high-frequency sound made by the spoken letter *S*, which frequently causes distortion. Sibilance is accentuated by the person speaking too closely into the microphone

Single-perf film—Film sprocketed on one side only

Single-system sound—A method of recording sound where the film recording the image also records the sound simultaneously along the edge by means of either a small optical or magnetic sound head within the camera

Skipping—A stroboscopic effect most commonly seen on the screen when the camera has panned rapidly over a scene. A picket fence or a line of trees will accentuate the effect

Slating—Identification of both picture and sound takes by use of the slate, or clapstick

Slow motion—The technique of slowing down action by shooting film at a rate (e.g., 48 fps) faster than the rate of projection (24 fps)

Sound dissolve—A simultaneous fading-in of one sound while fading-out another; also called a segue when applied to music

Sound log—A chart describing the various magnetic sound tracks for the mixer. The sound log is prepared by the editor, and marked with footage and cues

Speed of lens—The f/stop reading of a lens at its widest aperture

Split reel—A reel made up of two halves which separate to permit the use of film on cores

Sprocket holes—The perforations at the edge of film or magnetic stock which allow it to be transported in a precise frame-by-frame movement

Start mark—A mark made at the head of a work print and its associated magnetic sound tracks, which facilitates lining them up together for synchronous playback

Storyboard—A series of drawings and sound descriptions detailing the shot-by-shot structure of a film

Super 8—Film stock 8mm wide, the most commonly used amateur film gauge. The area of one frame of Super 8 is roughly one-third of a 16mm frame

Super 8 cartridge—A fifty-foot load of Super 8 film. The cartridge does not require manual threading but is simply inserted into the camera

Super—To superimpose two or more images on film so that they will appear on the screen simultaneously. This may be done by double exposure in those cameras which allow the film to be rolled back and reshot, but it is more commonly done in the lab during A & B roll printing, e.g., supering a title over a background scene. Specialized custom superimposition is done at an optical lab

Swish pan—A camera pan made so rapidly that the image is blurred

Sync pulse—An electrical impulse generated by the camera and transmitted to the tape recorder as a record of the camera's speed

Sync sound—Sound recorded simultaneously with picture in such a manner that it can be played back with the picture in a frame-to-frame relationship

Synchronizer—An editing device which allows a number of magnetic and/or picture tracks to be run together in a synchronous relationship

Synchronous motor—A camera motor which runs at constant sound speed, controlled by the 60-cycle pulse of the AC main lines

Synchronous sound—See sync sound

Synthesis—The relationship created when two or more shots are cut together, where each shot affects the meaning of the shots that precede and follow it

Tail—The end of a film or a piece of film footage

Tail slate—Slating, or identifying the take or film, at the end of a shot rather than at the beginning

Take—A shot, generally made with sound. If the same shot is made a number of times, the shots are called retakes, and recorded as take 1, take 2, take 3, etc.

Telephoto lens—Lenses with long focal lengths, usually 100mm and greater in 16mm, are called telephoto lenses. They have the capacity to make distant subjects seem close

Tilt—A vertical camera movement usually made while shooting from a tripod

Timing—The amount of light passing through the camera original when exposing a duplicate print determines the timing of a shot. The "Timer" is the man who sets the printing light

Tracking shot—A camera shot made by moving the camera alongside the action. In a studio the shot is normally made from a moving platform running on rails, or tracks, which have been laid in preparation for the shot

Transfer—The duplication of sound from 1/4-inch magnetic tape onto 16mm magnetic stock

Transport—The parts of the camera which move the film from the feed spool, through the intermittent movement at the gate, to the take-up spool

Tripod—A three-legged camera support

Tungsten-balanced film—Film made to be used with tungsten light of a standard color temperature (3200° K.) in order to produce realistic color

Tungsten light—Light produced by a tungsten filament

Tungsten rating—The rating of photographic lights or film in Kelvin degrees

Underexposure—Condition resulting when less light reaches the lens than is required to produce an image of medium brightness. Underexposure yields a dark image in which details are often lost

Viewfinder—An eyepiece and viewing system on the camera which allows the cameraman to see the shot as it will appear on film

Voice-over—An off-screen voice, usually a narrator's, heard on the sound track

Wild sound—Nonsynchronous sound recorded independently of picture, often at a different time or location from the actual shooting

Work print—A print made, with edge numbers, from the camera original and used for editing

Zoom lens—A lens with variable focal length

Zooming—Gradually changing the focal length of a zoom lens so that the camera appears to move closer to or pull away from the subject

INDEX